The Tudor Murder Files

For my mother, Philippa, who knows more than I ever will.

The Tudor Murder Files

James Moore

PEN & SWORD
HISTORY

First published in Great Britain in 2016 by
PEN AND SWORD HISTORY
an imprint of
Pen and Sword Books Ltd
47 Church Street
Barnsley
South Yorkshire S70 2AS

ISBN 978 1 47385 703 2

Typeset in Times New Roman by
CHIC GRAPHICS

Pen & Sword Books Ltd incorporates the imprints of Pen & Sword
Archaeology, Atlas, Aviation, Battleground, Discovery,
Family History, History, Maritime, Military, Naval, Politics, Railways,
Select, Social History, Transport, True Crime, Claymore Press,
Frontline Books, Leo Cooper, Praetorian Press, Remember When,
Seaforth Publishing and Wharncliffe.

For a complete list of Pen and Sword titles please contact
Pen and Sword Books Limited
47 Church Street, Barnsley, South Yorkshire, S70 2AS, England
E-mail: enquiries@pen-and-sword.co.uk
Website: www.pen-and-sword.co.uk

Contents

About the Author

James Moore is a freelance journalist and author, with a passion for exploring the lesser known parts of our past. He has written eight books, including four other popular history titles: *Murder at the Inn: A History of Crime in Britain's Pubs and Hotels; Pigeon-Guided Missiles and 49 Other Ideas That Never Took Off; Ye Olde Good Inn Guide: A Tudor Traveller's Guide to the Nation's Finest Taverns and History's Narrowest Escapes*. His journalistic work has appeared in many publications including the *Sunday Telegraph*, *Daily Express* and *Daily Mirror*. He lives in Gloucestershire with his wife, two sons and far too many books.

Acknowledgements

A book covering this much territory is only possible with the help and support of a large number of people. In particular I would like to thank: Tamsin Moore, Alex Moore, Laurie Moore, Philippa Moore, Sam Moore, Dr Tom Moore and Geoffrey Moore as well as Dr Claire Nesbitt, Lana Matile Moore, Sarah Sarkhel, Robert Smith, Samm Taylor, Laurence Heyworth, Jan Hebditch, Felicity Hebditch, Jim Addison, Daniel Simister, Will and Fiona Poole, Emma Price, Julia Murphy, Fran Bowden, Martin Phillips, Steph Eccles, Carol Trow and Heather Williams.

Front cover image
The murder of David Riccio, from The Murder of Rizzio, by John Opie, 1787. (Courtesy of the Guildhall Art Library)

Back cover image
Queen Elizabeth I, from an oil painting by Henry Gillard Glindoni. (Courtesy Wellcome Library, London)

Introduction

'Truth will come to light; murder cannot be hid long.'
The Merchant of Venice

Murder was much on the mind of William Shakespeare; he used the word more than 200 times in his plays. It would not have been surprising if the unlawful slaughter of his fellow man pre-occupied the bard, for during the era in which he lived the homicide rate was at least five times higher than it is today. The Tudor age, which began in 1485 with the reign of Henry VII and ended in 1603 with the death of Elizabeth I, was a dangerous and bloody one. Under Henry VIII alone there were 72,000 executions and the Tudor epoch has become synonymous with the beheadings of high profile figures like Anne Boleyn, Thomas Cromwell and Mary Queen of Scots. Yet it was also a time in which the everyday threat of murder was always present, whichever sector of society you came from. Sudden death at the hands of others could come in many forms: from the blade of a robber, the sword of a rival or deadly poison administered by a cheating spouse.

The crime of murder was one that filled the nation with a growing fear, but fascination too. There was a new eagerness among the public to know all the details of murder cases, with chroniclers and pamphleteers producing comprehensive accounts of the most sensational killings to a news-hungry audience. This book is written in that tradition, seeking to bring together all the most dramatic true life tales of murder from the reign of the Tudors for the first time. From stories of grisly domestic killings, to elaborate plots inspired by lust, as well as politically motivated assassinations, many of the cases throw up intriguing mysteries as well as providing powerful insights into social history.

The focus of the *Tudor Murder Files* is mainly on murders from England but also touches on some of the most shocking and compelling stories from Scotland and Wales. With a cast list that includes Sir Thomas More, Sir Francis Drake, Christopher Marlowe and many more, as well as a startling variety of motives, methods, culprits and victims this collection proves that when it comes to murder the Tudor period could serve up cases just as shocking and mysterious as those from our own times.

PART ONE:
MURDER AND THE TUDORS

The Deadly Deed

What was murder?

'Of all the felonies murder is the most heinous' so wrote the Elizabethan legal expert Sir Edward Coke. His contemporary, the writer Anthony Munday, branded it an 'abhominable offence in the sight of God and Man'. This did not mean that the Tudors thought that murder was the worst crime; that position was reserved for treason, which as well as including direct attempts to overthrow the monarch could even include counterfeiting. Felonies were defined as serious crimes where the punishment was usually death. In Tudor England, it was not only murder or treason that could see you executed – you could equally be hanged for offences such as rape or robbery.

By the 1500s it was established that murder was something carried out furtively with some form of pre-meditation. In *The Boke of Justyces of Peas*, published in 1510, murder was described as 'where a man by malice pre-pensed lies in wait to slay a man and according to that malicious intent and purpose he slays him so that he who is slain makes no defence.'

During the course of the sixteenth century, English law began to define the boundaries of murder more clearly. Someone who was an accessory to a murder, or who instigated one, became equally culpable even though they hadn't wielded a weapon. Beating a person or making someone else do so could be murder if the victim then died of their injuries. If a murderer planned to kill someone but happened to kill someone other than their intended target, it could still be murder. And, if a group set out with the intent to kill, they could all be tried for murder, even though they might not have committed the act themselves.

Murder was made distinct from manslaughter under the Tudors, with the latter defined as a death that occurred as a result of 'chance medley', essentially in a hot-blooded affray. The line between manslaughter and murder remained muddied, particularly in the case of sudden, apparently unpremeditated murders, during theft for instance. The penalty for manslaughter could still be death but the crime rarely ended in a hanging. When the playwright Ben Jonson killed actor Gabriel Spencer in a duel in 1598, he was tried for manslaughter and escaped execution.

Infanticide, the killing of newborn babies, had historically been dealt with by the separate ecclesiastical courts, but from the Tudor period, as worries grew about its prevalence, secular courts became involved. It filled Tudor commentators with horror. One pamphlet told of a maid 'delivered of a sweet and tender infant' but 'casting all motherly and natural affection from her buryed the same alive.' Infanticide carried the death penalty, but prosecutions were few as proof was needed that the baby had been born alive.

Witchcraft, used to kill, was treated as a separate felony from murder and in 1542 and 1563, acts of parliament were passed which decreed that anyone who used enchantment and sorcery to kill or destroy a person would be liable to the death penalty. Similar laws were enacted in Scotland. There were numerous cases. In 1566 Agnes Waterhouse, from Hatfield Peverel, was accused of bewitching to death William Fynne and was hanged. In 1593 Alice Samuel and her family were hanged for the killing of Lady Cromwell in Huntingdonshire and in 1594, Gwen Ellis was executed after causing the murder by witchcraft of Lewis ap John.

Suicide was seen as self-murder and, according to the Tudor writer William Harrison, writing in 1577, 'such as kill themselves are buried in the field with a stake driven through their bodies.'

From the outset of the Tudor period there was concern that murder and violence were on the rise. A statute of 1487 noted 'how murders and slaying … daily do increase in this land.' By Elizabeth I's reign, William Lambarde, a justice of the peace, despaired at the level of violence saying that 'sin of all sorts swarmeth'. While murder was not as rife as it had been in Medieval times, research by historians suggests that the chance of becoming the victim of a violent death in Tudor England was much higher than it is today. For example, the historian J.S. Cockburn calculated from court records that the homicide rate in Kent in the sixteenth century was 4.6 per 100,000 of the population. The rate in Essex was 6.8 per 100,000. This compares to a modern rate of around 1 per 100,000.

According to Edward Hext, an Elizabethan justice of the peace from

Somerset, one in five of all criminal cases never came before the authorities so, of course, many murderers may have remained undiscovered.

Culprits and victims

In a country with a population of no more than four million, made up of small and often rural communities, most murderers knew their victims. It is reckoned that thirteen per cent of all homicides occurred within families. Wives made up three quarters of the victims of domestic murder. There were occasional cases of children being murdered too, such as the woman from Kilburn who, 'with a peece of a billet brayned her two children'. Servants were often the victims as were, occasionally, masters and mistresses. Outside the home, men made up most of the victims of homicide, largely through fighting, with pre-meditated murder rarer.

Culprits were mostly men, but records suggest that by Elizabethan times as many as a quarter were women. Some murderers could prove seriously savage. In 1560, a Stratford cordwainer called George Hurte killed a woman in Leytonstone and also 'cut off her arms and legs.' Other murderers could show considerable cunning when it came to covering up their crimes. For example, in 1595 the landlady of an inn at Caythorpe in Lincolnshire smothered a wealthy guest, then cut his throat, leaving his hand on the knife, successfully making it look like suicide for four months, until a bloody smock sent for washing gave her away. Others showed less skill. In 1568, a woman who killed her stepdaughter moved the body three times, first burying it under a tree, then in a field of oats and finally throwing it in a pond.

Cases of convicted serial killers were almost unknown in sixteenth century England. It's likely that any Tudor serial killers that did exist were clever enough never to be brought to book for their crimes. One of those with the guile to avoid the reach of the law may have been Edward St Loe, an MP from Somerset who is believed to have poisoned his own wife and her first husband. He is also suspected of doing away with his own brother William in 1565, using the same method. William was married to Bess of Hardwick, often described as the wealthiest woman in Elizabethan England. She also fell ill, almost certainly having been poisoned by St Loe, but survived.

THE DEADLY DEED

Motives

Sex and extra-marital affairs gave rise to many murders, with pamphleteers of the day particularly pre-occupied with cases of women who engineered the deaths of their husbands in order to be with other men. One case from the 1550s involved a Warwickshire gentleman, Sir Walter Smith, who took a beautiful younger wife called Dorothy. In time her affections wandered and she took a lover, William Robinson. Desperate to be with him rather than her ageing spouse, Dorothy persuaded a groom and a maid to help her kill Smith. Together they strangled him with a towel in his bed. They got away with the crime for a couple of years until the groom blurted out what had happened whilst drunk. Convicted of murder at the Warwick assizes, he and the maid were hanged while Dorothy was burned at Wolvey Heath. Sexual jealousy could also lead to murder. In 1540, for example, James Rination was hanged in Moorfield, London, for murdering his master in a garden over a 'harlot'.

Financial gain has always been a strong motive for murder and the Tudor era was no different. One contemporary author spoke of how any man of means was fearful to reveal he had money lest it might 'abridge his days'. In July 1533, John Wolfe and his wife Alice lured two foreign merchants on to a boat in the Thames, where they proceeded to murder and rob them. In another case, John Graygoose and John Wright, who were married to the sister and mother of a Thomas Chambers, cooked up a plan to murder him before he came of age and inherited a large fortune from his father's estate, so that their families would benefit instead. Wright, a tanner from Upminster, killed Chambers in June 1595 but was later caught acting suspiciously and went to the gallows in Romford.

A few high profile murders were part of wider political intrigues such as the famous murder of Lord Darnley, the husband of Mary Queen of Scots (see page 108). There were less well known instances too. In 1542, Thomas Trahern was ambushed and slain on a road near Dunbar while on a diplomatic mission for Henry VIII to James V's court in Scotland. The three attackers used a dagger, lance and sword but were later apprehended and hanged. Henry blamed James for Trahern's death.

Among the gentry, feuds threw up occasional murders. In 1556 for example, a pair of warring families led George Darcy to murder Lewis West near Rotherham. Riots, rebellions and local grievances could lead to murder by the mob. In 1497, a tax collector in Taunton fell victim to a local rising while in October 1536, Dr John Raynes was dragged off his horse and killed in Horncastle during a riot, with some of the perpetrators later hanged. In 1548, Crown Commissioner William Body arrived to destroy Catholic relics in Helston church in Cornwall, but 3,000 angry locals turned out to oppose him. He ended up stabbed to death.

Sometimes the motive for murder utterly defied explanation. In 1572, Bristolian John Kynnestar was arrested for stabbing his wife in the heart twenty-five times. He told a constable that the idea to kill her came in a dream. It is likely he was suffering from some mental illness; this going unrecognised, he was hanged for the crime.

Methods of murder

According to Coke, murder might be committed 'by poyson, weapon sharp or blunt, gun, crossbow, crushing, bruising, smothering, suffocating, strangling, drowning, burning, burying, famishing, throwing down, inciting a dog or bear to bite' or even 'leaving a sick man in the cold.'

Hitting a victim with some form of blunt instrument was perhaps the most common method. This might be almost anything from a pestle and mortar, in the case of a Worcestershire murder, to a piece of a stile in an Essex killing. In the dying days of the Tudor dynasty, innkeeper Thomas Merry killed Robert Beech with fifteen blows of a hammer, then his servant Thomas Winchester with another seven, leaving the weapon sticking out of the latter's head.

Almost everyone in the sixteenth century would have owned or had access to a knife or dagger and so it was unsurprising that sharp instruments crop up frequently in homicides. Cockburn reports that in Kent, in the reign of Elizabeth I, bladed weapons accounted for thirty-seven per cent of violent deaths. They could be used for some truly gruesome crimes. In 1580, for instance, Richard Tod murdered Mistress Skinner for money using his hunting knife, while in the same year, Margaret Dorington killed Alice Fox by thrusting a knife 'up under her clothes'. In 1589 at Penshurst in Kent, Alice Smyth was stabbed in the neck by labourers Roland Meadow and Nicholas Gower. They then 'slit open her stomach and took from it an unborn child.'

Swords or rapiers crop up occasionally in cases of Tudor murder, usually involving the upper echelons of society. Other types of blades also feature. In a case from Worcester in 1576, a man used an axe to kill his own brother. In 1555, Bennett Smith was hanged for the murder of

Giles Rufford. Smith had paid two men, Francis Coniers and John Spencer, to kill him and supplied them with two 'javelins' with which to carry out the crime at Alconbury Weston near Huntingdon.

In third place behind blades and bludgeoning came strangulation or smothering, with the neck of victims often broken for good measure. A sly murderer might bet on the authorities not recognising the physical signs. Indeed, in 1582, when Thomas Cash from Holton in Lincolnshire strangled his wife Ellen to be with another woman, his spouse's ill health was blamed. He got away with the crime until 1604, when his mistress revealed his culpability on her deathbed. Cash later confessed.

Easy to administer and difficult to detect in an age before scientific post-mortems, poison was the most feared method of murder in the Tudor era. Arsenic seems to have been the most commonly used agent; often called ratsbane, it was readily available to buy in order to keep down vermin.

Poisoning struck fear into elite members of society as it was a weapon that could be used secretly, with women and servants especially thought to favour this cunning ploy to do away with husbands and masters. Coke called it the most hateful form of murder 'because it is most horrible and fearful to the nature of man'. In 1599, James VI of Scotland wrote that it was a crime a king was 'bound in conscience never to forgive'. Poisoning was difficult to prove but convictions were made. In 1571 Rebecca Chamber of Harrietsham in Kent was found to have poisoned her husband Thomas by giving him a wooden bowl containing 'roseacre and milk'. Christopher Bainbridge, Archbishop of York, died in Italy in July 1514, after his soup was poisoned by his own chaplain, Rinaldo de Modena.

Rumours of unproven poisonings gave rise to many mysteries. Was the food of Margaret Drummond, mistress of Scotland's James IV, purposely contaminated to ease his marriage to Margaret Tudor, daughter of Henry VII? Was Richard Clough, who died in Hamburg at the age of forty, poisoned because of his secret life as a spy for Elizabeth I?

Poison could have unintended consequences. In 1573, John Saunders of Warwickshire tried to poison his unsuspecting wife with an apple. She happened to give the deadly fruit to her three-year-old daughter instead of eating it and the girl died. Saunders was found guilty of murder, even though he had killed the wrong person.

Firearms were still novelties at the beginning of the Tudor period and notoriously inefficient. Yet as the sixteenth century wore on, worries about gun crime grew. During the reign of Henry VIII, there were measures to ban handguns with a 1541 statute bringing a clampdown following 'diverse detestable and shameful murders' involving them. Just two per cent of cases of homicide in Kent during the 1560s were caused by guns, but Elizabeth I's government sought to introduce more controls, with particular concern over the use of pocket pistols known as 'dags'. In 1575, the Privy Council complained of thieves armed with pistols who 'murder out of hand before they rob.'

The century saw the gun become a favourite weapon of the assassin. In 1570, the Regent Moray, ruling Scotland during James VI's minority, was gunned down from a window in Linlithgow as he passed in a cavalcade below. The killer was James Hamilton, who used a carbine to fire two lead balls into Moray's belly as he rode by. It's thought to have been the first ever political assassination using a firearm.

Catching and Convicting Murderers

In *Sundry Strange and Inhumane Murders*, a pamphlet detailing some of the worst crimes of the 1590s, the anonymous author wrote, 'Horror and fear always accompanieth the murderer ... he standeth in dread of every beast bush and bird ... God seldom or never leaveth murder unpunished' compelling the culprit to 'lay open the truth to the world'. There had been a belief, at least since the time of Geoffrey Chaucer, who first coined the phrase in his *Canterbury Tales*, that one way or another 'murder will out'.

This conviction was a useful one, given that in the sixteenth century there was no organised police force and arresting a murderer could be an extremely tricky business. This did not mean, however, that urgent action was not taken when a murder occurred or was suspected. In fact, the whole local community was expected to chip in and help bring the killer to justice. If a recent murder was discovered, assuming the suspect was not immediately apprehended, the 'hue and cry' would be raised. This practice dated back to the thirteenth century and required all able bodied men to down tools and join in the pursuit of the suspect. A whole community could be fined for not taking part.

The role of the humble parish constable, unpaid and appointed for a year by local aldermen, was important at this stage. William Harrison described how, after getting a warrant, it was his 'duty to raise the parish about him, and to search woods, groves, and all suspected houses and places, where the trespasser may be, or is supposed to lurk; and not finding him there, he is to give warning unto the next constable, and so one constable, after search made, to advertise another from parish to parish, till they come to the same where the offender is harboured and found.'

The hue and cry could be effective. In 1595, William Randolph, a grazier from Cardiff, was murdered near Aylesbury. Descriptions of the suspects, who had been seen acting suspiciously before Randolph's dead body was found in a thicket, helped track one of the culprits down to as far away as Wales.

Often, however, the burden of bringing a murder to the attention of the authorities fell on victims' families themselves. In 1580, Nicholas Turberville was murdered at Wells in Somerset by his brother-in-law, John Morgan, a 'lewd and wicked liver'. Despite 'lying in childbed' Turberville's wife 'arose and went to have law and justice pronounced on that cruel malefactor.' Morgan was hanged at Ilchester on 14 March.

Investigations

Constables and neighbours, mayors and other officials including the local sheriff, whose job was to oversee law and order in the county, could all become involved in initial murder enquiries. However, if a murder suspect was apprehended or suspected, sooner or later the matter would come before the local justices of the peace. These were magistrates usually chosen from among the ranks of the local gentry. Their main job was to hear lesser crimes at quarter sessions. While they would not usually try cases of murder, they were regularly involved in the job of ordering the search of properties, interrogating suspects, checking alibis and backgrounds, encouraging confessions and taking depositions from witnesses as well as ensuring that arrested suspects were delivered to gaol awaiting court proceedings. There was even advice issued to JPs advising them on what body language to look for in a guilty person.

In cases of suspicious death, the coroner would also be called for. The office of coroner had been established in the twelfth century and by the Tudor era, coroners had become very important in identifying murder suspects. Along with the justices of the peace they were, in effect, the nearest thing to a modern day detective. The coroner would first open an inquisition with a jury of at least twelve men, summoned by the sheriff or bailiff. He and his jury would then typically inspect the body of the victim, noting any wounds and trying to establish just how the victim had died. The coroner might be obliged to put their thumb into a wound to ascertain its nature and depth.

As well as identifying if the person had been murdered, the job of the coroner was to seek out the murder weapon and even give it a monetary value. Coroners could also examine witnesses, family members and suspects. In the case of the murdered hosier Abel Bourn, for example, the coroner was able to establish that the chief suspect, a man called Wood, could not come up with an alibi for what he had been doing on the day of the murder. Finally, the coroner would ask the jury to reach a verdict as to who might be responsible for a murder. Their findings would then be passed to court officials preparing indictments.

In the course of enquiries into a murder, supernatural forces could be called upon to help. Very common was the curious practice of bringing suspects in front of the corpse of the person they were alleged to have killed. If the dead body was observed to 'bleed afresh' in their presence then this was taken as a sign from God that they were responsible. For instance, when Thomas Hil of Faversham killed his own mother and had her buried before his brother could attend the funeral, his suspicious sibling insisted on the body being exhumed. Discovering no sign of the plague, from which the woman was supposed to have died, Hil was brought before the body where the corpse 'bled both at the nose and at the mouth; whereupon hee confessed.'

This is not to suggest that educated medical expertise was never sought during investigations. In December 1597, when the body of a barrister was found floating in the Thames, a group of learned surgeons gave their opinion that the dead man had met his end not by drowning but by suffocation. Suspicion fell upon Richard Aungier, his son, who was hanged for the murder a month later. In the case of Thomas Robinson (see page 168) a kind of post mortem was undertaken in which physicians were apparently able to identify that the victim had died through poisoning.

Examination of witnesses could be very thorough. In January 1577, Alice Neate, of Colchester in Essex, slit her sister in law's throat while she lay in bed. At first Alice's own daughter Abigail denied that her mother had anything to do with the crime but under 'straight examination' she was persuaded to reveal the truth – that Alice had done it. She knew because she was lying in bed awake in the same room and watched the whole thing. Alice was duly hanged.

Despite many thorough investigations, murderers were not always caught. Arrests were haphazard and, in practice, many constables, coroners and JPs were corrupted or dragged their feet if they had any personal interest in seeing a murder hushed up. Many murderers could simply not be found, even where their identities were known, with the suspects made outlaws.

Prisons and trials
While a murder suspect awaited trial he would usually languish, clamped

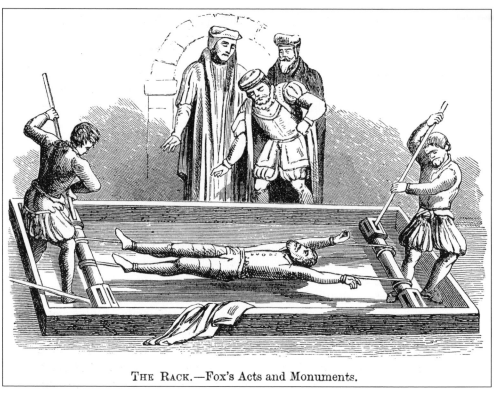

in irons, in a local gaol. This might be sentence enough; many prisoners died of disease, thanks to insanitary conditions. Some of the bigger prisons, particularly in London, became infamous. Here, murderers could find themselves awaiting justice at the King's Bench prison, the Fleet, Marshalsea, Newgate and just occasionally in the Tower of London itself. Here, although not officially sanctioned, confessions could be obtained by torture using the rack, a device that stretched out the victims' limbs inflicting extraordinary pain. According to Sir Walter Raleigh, the rack was 'used nowhere as in England'. Prisons were also places where condemned men would return after a conviction to await their execution. Here they might be visited by family or clergy encouraging them to repent.

Tudor trials, even for murder, were over in as little as half an hour and almost never lasted longer than a day. They were usually heard in front of crown-appointed judges at the twice-yearly travelling courts known as the assizes or in more regular sessions in London. Murder cases could also be heard or transferred to the superior court of the King's Bench at Westminster Hall in London, with members of the nobility tried by their peers.

Before a trial began a grand jury would study indictments prepared by a coroner or JP to see if there was a case to hear. If a bill of indictment was found to be 'true', the arraignment process would get under way, where the indictment would be read out and the prisoner would have the chance to plead. If the plea was guilty their case would be set aside for sentencing. If they pleaded not guilty they had the right to tried by 'God and the country' which in effect meant a jury of twelve men, comprised of gentlemen and yeomen.

The shackles of the prisoner were removed and the prosecution's case would be put forward with witnesses, including children, testifying under oath. Evidence would be presented, including the depositions made to justices of the peace, as well as any confession or statements made by the accused. The accused was not allowed legal representation but could speak on their own behalf and was sometimes allowed to present witnesses in their defence.

Juries were supposed to decide the case on its merits but were often given heavy direction by the judge and usually came up with a verdict in a matter of minutes. There's no doubt that if you had enough influence, juries, coroners and justices could all be leaned on to bring in lesser verdicts or acquittals.

This did not mean that trials were a mere formality. Indictments for murder might turn into convictions for manslaughter instead. Courts sometimes found defendants insane or, finding they had the wrong suspect, ascribed fictitious names to the unknown real culprits like 'John at Death'. Conviction rates varied wildly, from forty-nine per cent in Sussex to sixty-eight per cent in Kent, according to calculations by the historian John Bellamy.

If the prisoner was found guilty he could make a plea of leniency, perhaps claiming benefit of clergy (see below). If not, sentencing would proceed. Along with being executed, murderers could be subject to forfeiture of their goods, which would be seized by the crown, while the gentry could be stripped of their titles and lands. In some cases these might be redistributed or eventually given back to the families in question.

Forfeiture ensured that the sins of the fathers were revisited on their heirs.

If an indictment had not led to a conviction, or if a murder suspect had evaded the law, there was another way for a murderer to be brought to justice and that was to make an 'appeal' of murder. This was usually done by the victim's next of kin, often in cases where they felt justice might be obstructed by local bias. This was the case when John Pauncefote, a justice of the peace from Gloucestershire, was shot and murdered in 1516. He had been on his way to quarter sessions in Cirencester when attacked by a group of men including Sir John Savage, who was actually sheriff of Worcestershire. Pauncefote's widow made an appeal to the King's Bench. After much wrangling, Savage got a royal pardon but not before he had been ordered to pay Pauncefote's family considerable compensation. Thus 'appeal of felony' wasn't simply a path to justice but important financially for those who had lost a breadwinner.

Getting away with murder

If you wanted to get away with murder, or at least escape capital punishment, it helped to have God, or rather the Church, on your side. It also helped to be a man. Claiming 'benefit of clergy' meant that those in holy orders could be punished more leniently by the separate church courts. This privilege wasn't just for priests but effectively any man who could claim some link to the Church and demonstrate that they could read a portion of text in Latin.

Over time the right to benefit of clergy was restricted. In 1489, just four years into Henry VII's reign, a new statute stated that laymen could only claim the privilege once and must have the letter M branded on their thumb. Further interventions through the sixteenth century meant that benefit of clergy eventually stopped being used in murder cases. Women condemned to die for murder could avoid death temporarily, by claiming to be pregnant. If this was found to be true they were remanded until they gave birth and could sometimes escape the noose.

An individual who had committed murder could also flee to a church, or specific consecrated place and claim the ancient right of sanctuary - places deemed to be outside the jurisdiction of the secular law. There were a few monasteries where permanent sanctuary might be possible, but in most places the protection of the clergy lasted for forty days, after which time the criminal would usually have to face normal legal procedure.

In 1527, Thomas Parker fled to a Leicester church admitting: 'I have strykyn Thomas Otfield and gaff hym the wound wherof he died.' He claimed sanctuary in the hope of saving his life. Murderers like Parker could escape the noose if they admitted their crime to the coroner and agreed to 'abjure the realm' – leaving the country for good. They would be accompanied by the coroner to the nearest port, wearing no shoes and carrying a cross. Parker left England from Boston in Lincolnshire. From 1529, a letter 'A' was branded on to the abjurer's thumb in case they tried to come back. As Church and state tussled during the Reformation, attempts were made to curb criminal sanctuary and it was finally abolished under James I.

Royal pardons could often help murderers avoid the gallows, perhaps issued because the legal process was found to be lacking, new evidence had emerged or to an accessory who had provided information to help convict others. A person of high standing whose friends had the ear of the monarch might get a pardon or it could simply be granted because the sovereign wished to bestow favour on a high ranking individual he considered useful. One of those pardoned was Edmund de la Pole, Earl of Suffolk, who found himself arraigned at the King's Bench for murder in 1498 after he killed a man in a brawl.

In cases of feuding families, tit for tat murders could go unprosecuted. Others could get away with it simply by virtue of their social standing. Sir Thomas Salisbury, a JP in Denbighshire paid off a victim's relatives when one of his servants killed two men. In Scotland, when James Stewart, the 2nd Earl of Moray was murdered in Edinburgh his killer, the Earl of Huntly, was given merely a week's house arrest. Murderers could sometimes escape hanging if they made an arrangement with their victim's family. In 1599, a man agreed to forgive his brother's killer as long as the culprit was given twenty years' banishment.

Punishments

The Triple Tree at Tyburn, first set up in 1571, allowed more than one criminal to be hanged at the same time. (Copyright Look and Learn/Peter Jackson Collection)

Hanging

Once sentence of death had been passed by a Tudor court, punishment was swift. Executions normally occurred within a few days of the judgement. Often these would take place near the scene of the crime to demonstrate locally that justice had been done and as a warning to others. When Richard Newbold, a yeoman of the guard, killed a servant of Lord Willoughby in 1512, Henry VIII ordered that he be hanged in Westminster Palace itself and left there for two days as an example to all.

Hanging – by the neck until dead – was by far the most common form of execution for murder and had been so for about 400 years. Murderers would be escorted to a permanent or temporary gallows, usually consisting of two uprights and a crossbar, set up in a prominent place. Once the executioner had attached a condemned person to the noose, a cart or ladder would be pulled away, leaving them to swing. Each major town or city had their own gallows. In London it was Tyburn, on the road leading out of the city to the west (near today's Marble Arch) where murderers were most commonly hanged. It had been a traditional site of hangings since the twelfth century but in 1571, a new gallows was set up there which became known as Tyburn Tree. This triangular construction consisted of three 18ft wooden posts with 9ft crossbars. It could dispatch more than a dozen people simultaneously.

William Harrison considered hanging the most humane method of execution, citing it as the reason that condemned Englishmen 'doo go so cheerfullie to their deths.' In truth it was often a messy affair. Unlike the skilled hangmen of later centuries, Tudor executioners were amateurish. Death usually came slowly by strangulation rather than breaking of the neck. Sometimes there were extra punishments. In 1573, Peter Burchett ended up in prison after having stabbed and wounded the admiral Sir John Hawkins in a London street. Behind bars, Burchett managed to kill one of his keepers and was hanged for the murder in the Strand, but not before his right hand had been cut off and nailed to the scaffold.

Bodies were buried by the gallows themselves or 'hanged in chains'. This involved leaving an executed individual's corpse dangling in a public spot as a warning. Shooter's Hill, near London, was a favoured location for these macabre reminders, while in 1530, the murderer of a Dr Miles was hanged in chains at Finsbury Fields. The corpse could remain, gradually decomposing, for years. In *Of Sundry Kinds of Punishment*, published in 1587, William Harrison reported how a murderer might be 'hanged alive in chains near the place where the fact was committed … and so continueth till his bones consume to nothing.'

A public hanging was a carefully orchestrated spectacle and could attract thousands of onlookers. Executions were carried out with great fanfare, often with a number of felons being put to death at the same time to heighten the drama and carnival atmosphere. Murderers themselves were expected to enter into the spirit of it, confessing their sins to the crowd and asking God for mercy. Most did, but some defiantly refused, like Charles Gavaro, hanged at Smithfield in 1550 for killing two captains near Newgate. Others might induce sympathy among the crowd. In his *Chronicles of England, Scotland and Ireland*, Raphael Holinshed describes the hanging of a murderer, Philip Price, in London's Fleet Street in 1582. Price had killed one of the men who had arrested him for an unspecified crime, but was so repentant and tearful on the scaffold that with, 'his vehement sighs and greevous grones … he so mooved the beholders, that manie which beheld him, pitied his wofull end.'

A modern plaque at the spot where the Tyburn Tree stood, near today's Marble Arch in London. (Copyright James Moore)

Burning at the stake

Being burned at the stake had been, since Medieval times, a punishment associated with those who had been found guilty of heresy. Yet Tudor murderers could also be burned at the stake when convicted of 'petty treason', the name given to murderous acts committed against a superior. The reason that the word treason was attached to this was because it was considered worse than murder, in that it offended the Tudor idea of the natural order of society. It could be petty treason when a wife killed her husband or a servant killed their master or mistress. Men convicted of petty treason were drawn on a hurdle to the point of execution and hanged but, in a sign that Tudor society viewed such transgressions by women as especially loathsome, female killers were to be burned at the stake.

Witches were usually hanged, not burned, for their crimes in the Tudor years; it was murderesses who were consigned to the flames. In 1515, for example, a woman was burned in King's Lynn for murdering her husband while in 1582 there was a sensational case involving a Worcester man called Thomas Beast. His wife had an affair with one of his servants, Christopher Tomson, who was described in a pamphlet of the day as a 'lusty yonker'. She persuaded him to kill her spouse so they could be together, even organising the murder weapon for him. Tomson struck Thomas Beast with a forest bill (essentially a pole with a curved blade attached) while he was in a field. He didn't get far before he was apprehended and confessed to the crime, also revealing who had put him up to it. Both he and his lover were found guilty and executed. Mistress Beast was bound 'to a stake and the fire made to burne about her, her wretched carkas was soone dissolved into the ashes.'

If lucky, those condemned to be burned at the stake might be strangled first by having a cord tightened around their neck and the stake. If this didn't happen or didn't work, they would die from smoke inhalation as the faggots underneath them smouldered, or succumb in agony to the heat and flames.

Women found guilty of petty treason could be burned at the stake in England right up until 1790.

Pressed to death

This particularly gruesome punishment, known as 'peine forte et dure' had its origins in the Standing Mute act of 1275. This had ordered 'strong and hard imprisonment' for those not prepared to enter a plea of guilty or not guilty at their arraignment, because technically unless they did so they could not be tried. Initially, someone accused of a felony like murder, but who would not make themselves subject to a jury, was, in effect, starved in prison. But by the sixteenth century this had morphed into something more horrific – the practice of gradually placing heavy stones on the chest of the person accused. These were added until either the unfortunate soul expired or they decided to enter a plea after all.

In *De Republica Anglorum*, published in 1583, the English scholar Sir Thomas Smith painted a vivid picture of being pressed to death, a process which was undertaken inside a prison like Newgate. He described it as 'one of the cruellest deathes that may be,' going on to explain how 'he is layd upon a table, and another uppon him, and another weight of stones or lead laide upon that table, while as his bodie be crushed, and his life by that violence taken from him.' Another account related how the accused 'has a great weight of iron and stone laid upon him. His diet, till he dies, is of three morsels of barley bread without drink the next day; and if he lives beyond it, he has nothing daily, but as much foul water as he can drink … and that without any bread.'

It was hoped that the very threat of being subjected to pressing was enough to encourage a plea to be entered or even, possibly, to bring on a confession. Yet some people still actually opted for this gruesome end. Why? The usual reason lay in an attempt to secure a legacy for their families. As Smith explains, 'This death some strong and stout hearted man doth choose, for being not condemned of felonie, his bloud is not corrupted his lands nor goods confiscate.' So a few, especially those who knew they were probably going to be convicted anyway, put their dependants before their own pain. Lodowick Greville, for example, indicted in 1589 on a charge of murdering of one of his tenants, was one of these. He was duly pressed to death, but his son inherited his lands (see page 138).

The most infamous case of pressing during the sixteenth century involved Margaret Clitherow, the wife of a butcher, who was arrested for harbouring Catholic priests at her home in York. She opted not to plead so that there would be no trial and her children would not have to give evidence. She was pressed to death on 25 March, 1586. Astonishingly, the punishment of peine forte et dure was still in use in the eighteenth century and not formally abolished until 1772.

Boiled to death

Henry VIII has a reputation as a tyrant who had scores of his enemies beheaded. Yet, compared to some of his subjects, those who suffered decapitation could be considered to have got off lightly, for the king was personally instrumental in enshrining into law a hitherto little-used punishment, which surpassed all others in its ghastliness. Death by boiling was known as a punishment in Europe before the sixteenth century and seems to have been particularly favoured in cases of forgery as well as murder. Sometimes water was used, on other occasions a vat of oil.

It fell to the Tudors to enshrine the practice of boiling people to death into English law. The occasion which caused parliament to pass the Acte of Poysoning in 1531 at Henry's encouragement was the case of Richard Roose, a cook accused of murdering two people with a deadly broth (see page 51). The new law made poisoning an act of petty treason punishable

A portrait of King Henry VIII in the Royal Collection at Windsor, after Hans Holbein. (Courtesy of Wellcome Library, London)

by boiling, a fate which was handed down to Roose and a number of others in subsequent years. These grim executions were undertaken with the full public theatrics that the sixteenth century audience expected and expressed the passion which the monarch and many others felt about the fearful crime of poisoning. In fact, Henry may have been building on a custom which was already in use, if not with full legal sanction. *The Chronicle of the Grey Friars of London* logged how, in 1522, a poisoner was executed at Smithfield in London by being lowered on a chain into boiling water several times until he was scalded to death.

During Henry VIII's reign, the punishment was seized upon with enthusiasm. In the same year as Roose perished, a maid was boiled in the market place in King's Lynn, Norfolk for poisoning her mistress. The chronicler Charles Wriothesley referred to another case, recording that in March 1542, a maiden called Margaret Davie was boiled in Smithfield for poisoning three households in London.

Boiling was officially abolished as a punishment in 1547 during the reign of Edward VI, though in the 1570s, William Harrison was still noting that the penalty for someone who 'poisoneth a man' was being boiled to death in water or lead.

Broken on the wheel

Being broken on the wheel was a mixture of torture and capital punishment where the condemned individual would be tied, alive, to a wooden wheel in a spread eagle fashion. Their limbs would then be broken with a metal rod or other instrument. Once their bodies had been shattered, the condemned person would either be strangled, given a mortal blow or simply left to die in agony. There were variations in how this bizarre practice was carried out. Sometimes, for example, the wheel itself would be used to inflict the injuries. The wheel might also be paraded around town bearing its bludgeoned victim and once they were dead, it was often raised up on a pole still bearing the mangled corpse.

This peculiar and barbaric punishment was widely practiced across the continent in cases of murder and was still being used as late as the mid-nineteenth century in Prussia to punish assassins. While not favoured in Tudor England, it was in use in sixteenth century Scotland. In 1571, Captain Calder, found guilty of murdering the Earl of Lennox, then regent, was broken on the wheel 'after the manner of France'. In April 1591, the same fate was meted out to a common murderer, John Dickson, who had killed his father. Robert Weir, who helped Jean Kincaid murder her husband in 1600, faced the same bloody end (see page 182).

Beheading

Technically members of the nobility could be beheaded for committing murder but some were hanged like common murderers to make a point. In Yorkshire, the Halifax Gibbet, a kind of guillotine, was used for executing felons but primarily to despatch thieves. It inspired another device which first started being used in Scotland during the reign of Mary Queen of Scots. Known as the Maiden, the contraption was used to lop off the heads of murderers and other felons in Edinburgh. Ironically, the Earl of Morton, who first introduced the Maiden to Scotland, would become one of its victims, decapitated in June 1581 for his part in the murder of Lord Darnley (see page 112).

Reporting Murder

Court and coroner's records from the sixteenth century usually included only the briefest of details about any particular murder case and the verdict reached. There were sometimes more details to be gleaned from the chronicles of people such as Edward Hall, and later on in Raphael Holinshed's *Chronicles of England Scotland and Ireland*, published in 1577, or John Stow's *Annales of England*. From the Elizabethan era there was a new development which coincided with growing literacy among the populace. Murder pamphlets, also called chapbooks, were forerunners of today's tabloids and included lengthy reports of murders considered particularly sensational. The subjects were sometimes ordinary folk, but more often came from the gentry or merchant classes. The pamphlets are full of vivid descriptions and rarely spared readers gory details. In *Two Notorious Murders,* from 1595, for example, a victim's corpse is found in a ditch. We learn that 'worms crawled in his mouth, nose, ears and his whole body was puttresed.'

As well as details of the crime, pamphlets would often include long moralising or religious passages railing against the perils of lust or avarice. These often revealed the prevailing climate of the time, perhaps warning of the unscrupulous nature of Catholics or the devilish ways of women. Some were written in verse and they might also include a supposed confession from the criminal themselves.

Murder pamphlets were commonly produced within days of the crime and sometimes even before a trial. Cheaply printed and costing as little as two pence, they would be sold to the crowds at executions or in taverns, often read aloud to a gripped audience. Many pamphlets were actually skilfully written and some were penned by well-known men of the age, such as the playwright Thomas Kyd. Indeed, they could become the basis for popular plays, such as *Arden of Faversham*, a work which has sometimes been attributed to William Shakespeare himself; he certainly read the major chronicles and no doubt many of the murder pamphlets too. Perhaps they helped inspire him to pen lines such as these, from his play *Henry VI, Part III*:

Why, I can smile, and murder whiles I smile,
And cry 'Content' to that which grieves my heart,
And wet my cheeks with artificial tears,
And frame my face to all occasions.

A portrait of the playwright William Shakespeare by Gaspard Lavaster, 1807. Contemporary Tudor crimes inspired some of the bard's work. (Courtesy of Wellcome Library, London)

PART TWO:
THE CASE FILES

* * *

Chapter 1

A King in the Frame for Murder 1489

The Tudor era was borne out of a Royal murder mystery. In 1483 the twelve-year-old Edward V and his brother, the Duke of York, aged nine, disappeared. It is generally believed that the Princes were slaughtered that summer. The usual suspect for ordering their untimely demise is Richard III, who had already declared their claim to the throne to be illegitimate and seized the crown for himself. Last seen playing in the grounds of the Tower of London, where they had been imprisoned, Richard is thought to have wanted the Princes out of the way so he could secure his position. Their bodies were never found. According to Sir Thomas More, writing thirty years later, the blue blooded pair were smothered to death on the orders of one of Richard's henchmen, Sir James Tyrell. More alleged that Tyrell had confessed to the crime before his execution for treason in 1502.

There are, however, other serious suspects for the alleged murder. Chief among these is Henry VII, who became the first Tudor monarch in 1485 following Richard's defeat and death at the Battle of Bosworth. The theory goes that Richard only became the accepted culprit as the result of later Tudor propaganda. Henry certainly had just as much to gain by the murder of the Princes as Richard. His own claim to throne was even more tenuous. While Henry was not in England between 1483 and 1485,

Royal murderer? An engraving of Henry VII by James Hulett, after George
Vertue. (Courtesy of Wellcome Library, London)

it is possible that the Princes had survived Richard's reign and were actually killed on Henry's orders, probably sometime in 1486. It was only then, well after he had become king, that Henry let it be known that the Princes had been murdered.

Henry's possible involvement in history's most infamous murders remains contentious, but there are suggestions that he may also have been implicated in another murder that is less well known, one which would help him tighten his grip on the country in the fledgling years of the Tudor dynasty.

The saying goes that nothing is more certain in life than death and taxes. This was never more true than in the case of Henry Percy, the fourth Earl of Northumberland, slain by a man apparently incensed by the swingeing levies being imposed to pay for Henry VII's foreign wars. Until his death, Northumberland had led a relatively charmed life. His father had supported the House of Lancaster in the Wars of the Roses and after he was killed his son was briefly imprisoned in the Tower. Working his way back into the favour of the Yorkist Edward IV, Northumberland's title was eventually restored and he was given important posts in the north of England. Despite drawing up his forces in support of Richard III at the Battle of Bosworth in August 1485, Northumberland mysteriously failed to commit them, helping to assure that the future Henry VII would be victorious and become king. Initially arrested after the battle, Northumberland was soon brought into the fold of the new regime and retained his offices in the north of England. Yet, at the start of his reign, Henry still saw the Earl as a potential threat. He was a powerful figure in Northumberland and Yorkshire, which had been Richard III's power base. For his part, however, Northumberland seems to have shown nothing but loyalty to the new sovereign.

In January 1489, Henry demanded huge new taxes in his military campaign to support independent Brittany against the French. It fell to the Earl of Northumberland to try and enforce the taxes in the North. But pro-Yorkist sentiment had lingered in the region and its citizens resented the new duties which ordered that every man pay the 'tenth penye of his goodes'. Northumberland warned Henry that the people were not able to pay the 'houge some requyred of them … nor yet would once consente to pay'. Henry refused to consider any concessions.

In April 1489, open rebellion broke out. One of those who vehemently opposed the king's taxes was a 'simple fellow' called John a Chambre who became one of the leaders of a rebel force, largely made up of commoners, which gathered in the vicinity around Thirsk. On 28 April, Northumberland and his entourage arrived at Cocklodge, his house in the area, in order to meet them. Northumberland had asked one of his followers, Sir Robert Plumpton, to bring a large company of men with 'bowes and arrowes'. Yet it seems he did not intend a violent confrontation. Perhaps unwisely, he approached the protestors unarmed. The chroniclers tell us that he, 'with faire wordes sought to appease, but they like unreasonable vilains, aledging all the fault to be in him, as chiefe author of the taxe' became enraged. John a Chambre and his men suddenly set upon the Earl and 'furiouslye and cruelly murthered bothe hym and dyvers of hys housholde servaunts.' The murder of an Earl at the hands of commoners shocked the nation, with Tudor chronicler William Peeris branding it a 'horrible mischief' and 'cruell cryme'.

Contemporary writers were also surprised that Northumberland's own armed retinue – numbering as many as 800 souls – had apparently not intervened to save him as he talked to the rebels. Peeris spoke of the treachery of those 'to whom he gave fees and was right speciall lord.' The poet John Skelton bemoaned their lack of action alleging that 'if they had occupied their spere and their shilde' then 'this noble man doubtles had not been slayne.' Skelton believed Northumberland's men 'held with the commones under a cloke'.

Had someone told them to hold back? According to the chronicler Edward Hall's account of the incident, Northumberland's murder had not been due to a sudden moment of madness on the part of a few rebels but had been 'procured'. In other words it had been planned in advance.

After the murder, the rebels grew in confidence and a new leader, Sir John Egremont, emerged. The city of York quickly came under their control. In response, Henry despatched a huge force of 8,000 men under the Earl of Surrey and, in the face of overwhelming opposition, the rebels dispersed without a battle. The Yorkshire Rebellion was over as quickly as it had begun and Northumberland, along with a handful of his servants, were the only ones to perish. John a Chambre was soon apprehended and that summer was hanged, 'upon a gibbet set upon a square paire of gallows lyke an arche traytoure and his complyces and lewde disciples were hanged on the lower gallows roude about their mayster.' Egremont escaped to France, while Northumberland was buried at Beverley Minster with due ceremony.

The result of the whole episode really could not have been better for the king. The Earl's death was useful in robbing the Yorkist opposition in the north of a potential leader. It also helped that the dead Earl's son was only eleven years old at the time, which meant that, for the time being at least, his father's lands fell into the king's hands. Meanwhile, Henry was able to appoint a man from the south, the Earl of Surrey, to shore up Tudor dominance over the northern part of the country, effectively quelling revolt. In the aftermath of the rebellion, Henry VII himself visited York to oversee the thorough implementation of the tax.

So did Henry have a hand in Northumberland's murder? Closer examination of the backgrounds of the two key men involved in the rebellion is revealing. John a Chambre does not seem to have been a staunch Yorkist or even a local, possibly originating from Wales. He was a Royal Forester at Galtres in the North Riding and had been given his position, for life, in recognition of his services fighting at Bosworth for Henry Tudor. Is it possible that he had been encouraged by the king's agents to believe he had something to gain from confronting Northumberland and was hurriedly hanged once the Earl was dead so he could not reveal who had put him up to it? Intriguingly, Egremont was actually Northumberland's cousin. As an illegitimate member of the Percy family he may have had a personal axe to grind against Northumberland. Most tellingly, after a brief period of exile on the continent, he quietly re-entered England and was given two manors in Northumberland by the king.

Even if Henry had not directly ordered the murder he had certainly left Northumberland vulnerable, purposely putting him at odds with those who might naturally have been his supporters. Northumberland had been left to the mercy of the mob and his death was, at the very least, suspiciously convenient.

There would be an uneasy relationship between the Percy family and the Tudors during the course of the next century. The fifth Earl never regained the offices or power his father had enjoyed. The brother of the sixth Earl was hanged for treason at Tyburn and the seventh Earl was beheaded at York after leading the failed Rising of the North in the reign of Elizabeth. The eighth Earl ended up in the Tower of London for his role in trying to help Mary Queen of Scots escape her imprisonment in England. In June 1585 he was found dead in his cell, apparently having shot himself with a pistol that had been delivered to him in a cold pie. The official inquest's verdict was suicide, but there were rumours that he had been murdered, with Sir Walter Raleigh one of those convinced that the Earl had not died of natural causes. A Star Chamber inquiry into the matter, made up of the queen's privy councillors, was convened. It also concluded that the Earl had taken his own life. A similar case of a supposed suicide behind bars would lead to even louder cries of murder in the reign of Henry VII's son, just five years into the new king's reign.

Chapter 2

Murder Made to Look Like Suicide 1514

The death of an infant child is always devastating for the parents in question, but when London merchant Richard Hunne's baby son Stephen passed away in March 1511, the consequences would end up shaking the whole of Tudor society. Given the heartache Hunne must have felt at the death of his five-week-old child it was, perhaps, not surprising that when Thomas Dryfield, the local parish priest at St Mary Matfelon in Whitechapel, demanded Stephen's christening robe in return for his services he was a little put out. The priest was following the custom of extracting a so called mortuary fee applied by the clergy when someone died, effectively as payment for the burial. Mortuary fees were regarded by some as not only insensitive, but symptomatic of a corrupt church feathering its own nest. Hunne decided to make a stand by refusing to give the priest his fee, claiming that as the piece of cloth was his and not his son's property, he was not obliged to part with it. For a time the matter was forgotten, but when Hunne and the church once again came into conflict the issue was revisited and would eventually have deadly ramifications.

Hunne lived in the parish of St Margaret's, London. He was a liveryman at the Merchant Taylors Company and was worth 'at least a thousand marks' according to the contemporary writer Thomas More, while the chronicler Edward Hall said he was 'of honest reputation, no man to the sight of people more vertuous.' Along with the mortuary issue Hunne came within the sights of the clergy over other issues. He had come to the defence of a neighbour called Joan Baker, who had been accused of heresy. Then, in November 1511, Hunne came into dispute with the parson of St Michael Cornhill over the title of a burnt out property.

The church was cracking down on Lollards, a group of dissenters who thought that the church should get back to the business of saving souls, rather than accruing wealth. Hunne was suspected of Lollardy, probably correctly. To send a message that Hunne's perceived attacks on the powers of the church were not acceptable, the matter of the unpaid mortuary fee was now pursued after all. In April 1512, probably encouraged by his superiors, Dryfield sued Hunne at the archbishop's Court of Audience held at Lambeth Palace – a higher level of church court than was strictly necessary. The judgement went against Hunne.

He, however, was not prepared to capitulate, refusing to hand over the robe or the six shillings and eight pence it was worth. Then, on 27 December, somewhat provocatively, he attended vespers at St Mary's. When the officiating chaplain, Henry Marshall, saw him, he refused to continue with the service unless Hunne left, calling out: 'Hunne, thou art accursed and standest accursed.' In January 1513, Hunne took a suit out against Marshall for slander at the court of the King's Bench, claiming his reputation as a businessman had been dented by the chaplain's remarks. He also took out a second action using the law of praemunire – claiming that the church had overstepped its authority in pursuing him for the mortuary fee.

The ecclesiastical authorities began to take the threat posed by Hunne's use of praemunire seriously. Originally intended to curb the power of the Pope in English matters it was now being more commonly used to challenge the Church's jurisdiction in ordinary legal cases. However, for several months there was a lull, with a series of adjournments as debate raged about the merits of each side's case. Then, in early 1514, in an attempt to outflank its enemies, the Church suddenly decided to begin proceedings against Hunne for heresy. In October, the Bishop of London, Richard Fitzjames, had the merchant arrested and a search made of his lodgings. Damning evidence was supposedly found, including the possession of a supressed bible in English. Hunne was thrown in the Lollards' Tower at St Paul's, a small prison attached to the cathedral.

Writing fifteen years later, Thomas More alleged that the Church had been right to pursue Hunne as he was indeed a heretic who had been attending subversive meetings. But the anti-clerical Edward Hall said that the priests did so out of 'malice' in revenge for the cases taken out against them. John Foxe in his *Actes and Monuments* says that the pre-Reformation Church wanted to make an example of Hunne to avoid more cases of praemunire being taken out.

On 2 December, Fitzjames interrogated Hunne at Fulham Palace.

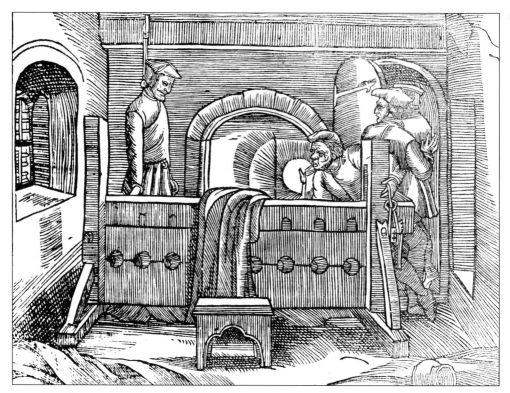

Murder or suicide? A woodcut from a 17th century edition of *Acts and Monuments* by John Foxe, showing the body of Richard Hunne discovered in the Lollards Tower at St Paul's Cathedral, London. (Courtesy of the Pitts Theology Library, Candler School of Theology, Emory University)

According to Foxe, Hunne was accused of both preaching and publishing against the laws of Almighty God, had spoken against the right of the church to collect tithes and likened the bishops and priests to 'the scribes and Pharisees that did crucify Christ'. There is evidence that Hunne made a partial confession that day but whatever he might have admitted to, it wasn't enough to satisfy Fitzjames and he was taken back to prison at St Paul's in the charge of Dr William Horsey, the bishop's chancellor.

On the morning of Monday 4 December, Hunne was dramatically found dead in his cell hanging from a beam. As soon as word of the death got out there 'arose great contention'. Dr Horsey let it be known that Hunne had simply committed suicide, but there was soon a clamour for justice among the citizens of London as rumours spread that Hunne had, in fact, been murdered.

The following day the coroner, Thomas Barnwell, and members of an inquest jury 'elected by great dyscrecion' went to inspect Hunne's body, which was still hanging in the cell. A pamphlet printed in the 1530s fleshed out the details of what they found. Hunne was 'hanging upon a staple of iron in a girdle of silke, with faire countenance, his head faire kemmed, and his bonet right sitting upon his head.' They observed that Hunne's eyes and mouth were closed, 'without any staring, gaping, or frowning, also without any driveling or spurging in any place of his body.' As some members of the jury took Hunne's body down they noticed that, strangely, the noose around his neck was loose. There was little blood on the body apart from some small streams coming out of his nose. The account continues, 'Save onely these foure drops of blood, the face, lips, chinne, doublet, coller, and shirt of the said Hun, was cleane from any blood.' They noted that Hunne's hands were free but marks on his wrists showed they had previously been bound.

Meanwhile, ignoring the uproar which was sweeping London, the Church risked more ire by proceeding with the case against Hunne for heresy despite the fact that he was already dead. This time the allegations included the claim that he had called the Pope 'Satan'. Over the course of a week a string of witnesses were produced to testify in front of three bishops that Hunne had engaged in heretical practices. And, on 16 December, Hunne's mouldering body was brought into the Chapel of Our Lady at the old St Paul's and put on trial. Hunne was found guilty. The final indignity came on 20 December when the Church, as was their right, had the city's authorities take Hunne's body to Smithfield where it was publicly burned at the stake.

While this was going on, the inquest into Hunne's death was also continuing. Over the coming weeks, its members found plenty of evidence which tallied with their growing suspicion that Hunne had been murdered rather than committed suicide. They concluded that the only thing in the room Hunne could have used to hang himself was a stool but it was in the wrong place. The girdle was too short for Hunne to have used it to hang himself and marks on his neck seemed to have been caused by something metal – perhaps a chain. The absence of the kind of bodily discharges usually associated with slow strangulation was also puzzling. Then there was the matter of a large pool of blood, found in a different part of the room from where the body hung. Added to this was the issue of Hunne's jacket which was covered in blood but folded down away from the body, 'which thing' they said Hunne could never 'doe after he was hanged.' Everything pointed to a crime and the inquest recorded that, 'it appeareth plainely to us all, that the necke of Hun was broken, and the great plenty of blood was shed before he was hanged.' Hunne, it seemed, had not only been murdered but hurriedly trussed up to make it look as if he had hanged himself.

The hunt was on for Hunne's killers and the authorities were helped in their endeavours by the behaviour of one of the chief suspects, the Bishop of London's 'summoner', Charles Joseph. Shortly after Hunne's body was discovered he had attracted suspicion by fleeing the capital, seeking sanctuary in the village of Good Easter in Essex. He was apprehended there and brought to the Tower of London, soon confessing that around midnight on the night that Hunne had died he, along with the bellringer John Spalding and Dr Horsey had climbed the staircase that led to the cell where they found the prisoner lying on his bed. Horsey had cried 'Lay hands on the thief' and the trio had then set about murdering Hunne. He stated that 'I, Charles, put the girdle about Hunne's neck. And then John Bellringer and I, Charles did heave up Hunne, and Master Chancellor pulled the girdle over the staple. And so Hunne was hanged.'

Joseph's confession, together with deposition from other witnesses taken by the inquest (at least as set down in the pamphlet), began to build up a picture of how events had unfolded. After Hunne had been brought back from his audience with Fitzjames on Saturday 3 December, Horsey had evidently come to Hunne praying forgiveness of 'all that he had done to him, and must doe to him.' Hunne spent most of that day locked in the stocks in his cell and later Spalding bound his wrists behind him before leaving him locked up. Meanwhile Joseph had gone to a brothel out of town, making sure to be seen by witnesses in order, it was believed, to give him an alibi. But that evening, under the cover of darkness, he had snuck back into London.

Later that night he entered Hunne's cell with Spalding and Horsey and put a wire, heated by the flame of a burning candle, up Hunne's nose. This may have had the intention of piercing Hunne's brain while leaving no marks, but it did not kill him as was hoped merely making him bleed profusely, accounting for the blood on his jacket. They then strangled him, possibly with a piece of chain. Hunne was hurriedly dressed in clean clothes before being lifted into the noose, made out of his belt, which was attached to a hook in the wall. For good measure, the murderers put Hunne's cap on his head and also brushed his hair.

Despite his efforts, Joseph had been spotted in London on Sunday evening and been seen around the Lollards' Tower on the Monday morning in a state of some agitation by three different people. For his part, Spalding had claimed not to have been at the prison that night but other testimony showed this to be a lie. He had shown other witnesses that he had the keys early on the morning that Hunne was later found dead. Among the many other pieces of evidence, one of Joseph's servants said that, two days after Hunne's body was found, her master had declared: 'I have destroyed Richard Hunne'.

Hunne's body had been found late on the Monday morning by assistant prison keeper Peter Turner. He had arrived to serve the prisoner breakfast at 8am but could not find Spalding. He was eventually brought the keys by one of the latter's underlings. When he and two others went up to the cell they found Hunne hanging, immediately informing Horsey who had rushed to view the spectacle accompanied by a host of other clergy.

The case was considered so sensitive that the King's Council and the sovereign himself took an interest. They undoubtedly had a hand in the progress of the inquest. Months went by before the coroner was allowed to produce his report, but the findings were no less sensational for the delay. The official document recorded that Joseph, Spalding and Horsey had 'felonioiusly strangled and smothered' Richard Hunne at the Lollards' Tower and 'also the neck they did break of the said Richard Hunne, and there feloniously slew him and murdered him'. It added that 'with the proper girdle of the same Richard Hunne of silk, black of colour, of the value of 12 pence, after his death, upon a hook driven into a piece of timber in the wall of the prison aforesaid, made fast and so hanged him.'

But could the three suspects successfully be brought to trial? Not if Fitzjames had anything to do with it. Horsey, along with the other two suspects, were certainly kept in custody awaiting proceedings. But in early 1515, Fitzjames branded the inquest jurors 'false, perjured caitiffs'. That spring he wrote to Cardinal Wolsey, denouncing the 'untrue quest' which had landed his chancellor with an indictment for murder, going on to maintain that Horsey was as 'innocent as Abel'. He also alleged that Charles Joseph's confession had been extracted through torture. Meanwhile, in response to the issue of clerical powers that had arisen, King Henry had ordered a whole conference in which the rights and wrongs of the case were hotly debated by councillors, MPs and churchmen.

In the end, a kind of fudge was arranged. In November 1515, despite Horsey's indictment for murder, Henry VIII himself instructed his attorney Sir John Earnley to accept the chancellor's plea of not guilty when the case came in front of the King's Bench. Horsey, incidentally, had submitted himself for trial even though, technically, he could have asked to be dealt with by the church courts. Thanks to the king, the case against Horsey was dismissed and it is thought that Joseph and Spalding also escaped any severe punishment.

It was not the end of the matter. The fact that no one had been brought to justice for what most still believed to be a murder rankled with many leading figures in non-ecclesiastical circles. In May 1523, after an appeal from Hunne's daughter Margaret and her husband Roger, parliament passed a bill ordering that Richard Hunne's property should be given back to his family. The king wrote to Horsey demanding that it should be he that recompensed Hunne's family and not the Royal purse that should suffer. In the letter he states that, despite pardoning Horsey for the crime, he still considers him guilty of it. He speaks of 'the murder cruelly committed by you ... as by our own records more at large plainly it doth appear'.

The king's apparent volte-face only left the matter of whether Hunne really was murdered even more open to debate. Thomas More, writing in *A Dialogue Concerning Heresies*, published in 1529, was convinced that he had committed suicide just as the Church had maintained. More, a fierce defender of the pre-Reformation Church, thought the witness testimony shaky and said that Hunne had hanged himself in despair. The Protestant Foxe, on the other hand, thought that the brave Hunne had been cruelly killed for making a stand, pronouncing him a martyr.

Many writers have pointed out that the Church really had no need to murder Hunne. Their heresy case was almost bound to succeed whereas murdering Hunne was likely to cause a backlash. But it is equally possible that the Church was worried that leaving Hunne alive any longer would only encourage a greater diminution of its powers and was prepared to resort to skulduggery.

One deposition, from Thomas Granger, a servant of the Bishop of London who was with Spalding on the Sunday evening, was at odds with the rest. He said that Hunne had asked for a knife saying he'd rather kill

A portrait of Sir Thomas More, who believed Richard Hunne hanged himself. Engraving by Jacobus Houbraken, after Hans Holbein the Younger. (Courtesy Wellcome Library, London)

himself than be treated so. However, if even half the rest of the evidence given to the inquest (and even More admitted that jurors must have been 'right honest menne') was real, then Hunne's death seems suspicious. As much as the Church didn't need to kill him, there was no reason for Hunne to have taken his own life. While he may have opposed the Church on some matters, he was still religious and would have considered suicide a sin.

Another theory is that Hunne may have been killed by accident during torture and that Horsey and his associates then tried to cover up their bungling. Death caused by over-zealousness is not out of the question, though it doesn't fully address the suspicious actions recorded by the witnesses. More plausible is that one of the three accused, most likely Joseph, not understanding the wider issues at stake, simply overstepped his authority. Fitzjames was then left to clear up the mess, having Hunne burned as a way of trying to deflect attention on to the victim's heretical views rather than the Church's responsibility for his death.

Many historians have viewed the Hunne affair as an early example of the rift between Henry and the Church that would explode a decade or more later. In the short term however, the Church weathered the storm and there is little evidence that the king was looking for a showdown at this time. It was, of course, really the issue of Henry's marriage that would see him begin a concerted campaign to rein in the powers of the Church. Mortuary fees were curbed, though not abolished, in 1530.

If none of the big political players had emerged a winner from the Hunne affair, then neither did those more intimately involved. Clearly deemed an embarrassment, Horsey was exiled from London to Exeter and died in relative poverty in 1543. Despite the king's directions, Hunne's family does not appear to have fully regained its fortunes either. By the late 1530s, his daughter Margaret was appealing to Thomas Cromwell claiming that she, her husband and her seven children were suffering extreme 'indigence and poverty'.

Chapter 3

Strangled with a Scarf, then Burned in an Oven 1518

Today, Farleigh Castle is a crumbling, romantic ruin standing in the quiet Somerset countryside. In Tudor times, as a fortified manor, it was an impressive sight described by the antiquary John Leland as both 'pretty' and 'stately'. Yet the history of its occupants during the sixteenth century was far from serene. Back then Farleigh was a hotbed of marital disharmony, domestic cruelty and murder. Five hundred years on, its tumbled down stones seem a metaphor for the many human lives wrecked by their association with the place.

In 1539, Lady Elizabeth Hungerford secretly wrote a long, plaintive letter to Henry VIII's chief minster Thomas Cromwell from the castle. She was married to Farleigh's owner, Sir Walter Hungerford, who had become a close ally of Cromwell's during that decade. Elizabeth's desperate missive told how she had been imprisoned by her own husband in a tower of the castle after he had unsuccessfully tried to divorce her. Not only had she been locked up, Elizabeth claimed, but Walter had endeavoured to have her starved to death and poisoned too. 'And so I am your most wofulst and poorest bed woman left in worst case than ever I was, as a prisoner alone, continually lockt in one of my Lord's Towers of his castell in Hungerford as I have byn these thre or four yers past, without comfort of any creature and under the custodie of my Lord's Chaplain… which hath once or twese heretofore poysond me…'

In the letter, smuggled out without Walter's knowledge, Elizabeth went on to protest that she had so often been denied nourishment that she had been forced to drink 'myne owne water or else I should die for lacke of sustenance.'

Determined to further his political career at any cost, Walter had found his wife an embarrassing burden following the sudden fall from grace of her once well-connected father, Baron Hussey of Sleaford. In 1536, Hussey had been beheaded at Lincoln as punishment for his association with the Pilgrimage of Grace, an uprising against Henry VIII which had been ruthlessly put down. Ironically, it had been Hussey who had originally helped Walter Hungerford climb the greasy pole, smoothing the way with Cromwell, as Walter was first made sheriff of Wiltshire in 1533 and then Lord Heytesbury in 1536.

Perhaps it was Walter's upbringing and early influences that were to blame for his brutal treatment of Elizabeth. For, when Walter was about fifteen, his step-mother, Agnes, had been responsible for arranging a fiendish murder. What is more her husband, Sir Edward Hungerford, Walter's father, may well have been in on the scheme too, or at least had a part in trying to cover up the killing.

Nothing is known about Agnes' background, apart from the fact that in 1518 she was already married to a man called John Cotell. It is thought that the couple were reasonably well to do and perhaps in the employment of the Hungerfords. In any case, in that year, Cotell mysteriously disappeared while at Farleigh. Just six months later, Agnes was married to Sir Edward Hungerford (who was recently widowed) and living at Farleigh Castle.

Sir Edward was an important man. He had been knighted as a soldier serving Henry VIII in France and had since become Sheriff of Wiltshire, Somerset and Dorset. But, just three years into his new marriage to Agnes, he died. The death came on the 24 January, 1522, just six weeks after he had made a will, dated 14 December, 1521, which stated that, 'the residue of all my goods, chatells, juells, plate, harnesse and all other moveables whatsoever they be I freely give and bequeath to Agnes Hungerford my wife.'

Agnes was not to benefit from these riches for long. In a matter of months she was being accused of murdering her former husband, John Cotell. On 25 August, 1522, she was brought before justices at Ilchester and indicted along with two of her servants, William Mathewe and William Inges. The court heard that the men were responsible for the death of Cotell, on 26 July, 1518, at the castle, by the 'procurement and abetting of Agnes Hungerford'.

On the day of the murder, Mathewe and Inges were said to have taken 'a certain linen scarf called a kerchier which the aforesaid ... then and there held in their hands, put round the neck of the aforesaid John Cotell, and with the aforesaid linen scarf ... did feloniously throttle, suffocate and strangle, so that the aforesaid John Cotell immediately died.' The indictment goes on to relate that they 'then and there put into a certain fire in the furnace of the kitchen in the Castle of Farley ... the body of the same John' which 'did burn and consume' it. This was all done, the court heard, with the knowledge and indeed at the behest of Agnes who gave 'comfort and aid to the actual murderers.'

Imprisoned in the Tower of London, Agnes and her conspirators were brought for full trial at Westminster on 27 November, where they all pleaded not guilty. However, the jury decided that they had indeed been to blame and sentenced all three to death. Agnes was hanged at Tyburn on 20 February, 1523. *The Chronicle of the Grey Friars* recorded that she had been, 'lede from the Tower un-to-Holborne, and there put into a carte at the church yerde' and 'so carred un to Tyborne' and there 'hanged'.

Interestingly, Agnes was not burned at the stake as women who murdered their husbands usually were. Perhaps this was a concession made due to her status. However, in accordance with practice, Agnes' possessions were seized by the crown. Mathewe was hanged alongside Agnes but William Inges sought 'benefit of clergy' (see page 14), claiming to be a clerk. This was denied, pending confirmation that he was, in fact, a bigamist. Six months later he too perished on the gallows.

Sadly, the existing records do not reveal why Agnes might have wanted to kill John Cotell or how she came to be married to Edward Hungerford quite so quickly afterwards. There are some intriguing possibilities, however, thrown up by examination of the known facts.

The speed of Agnes' union with Hungerford suggests that the two were already romantically involved by the time of Cotell's death. It seems probable that Agnes planned to ditch one husband for another who was further up the social ladder. Perhaps Hungerford had a hand in the murder too and that was one of the reasons why his wife was not arrested earlier. Certainly the swiftness with which the wheels of justice began to swing into action after Hungerford's death suggests that rumours about Agnes' murky past had been circulating for some time. The murder may well have been as good as common knowledge. But, holding the position of Sheriff, it is possible that Hungerford may have been able to shield his wife from prosecution while he was alive. Indeed, if there was a suspicion that he had been involved too, the authorities might have turned a blind eye given his connections to the royal court. Once Hungerford was dead, however, they saw the way clear to pursue the matter, perhaps now spurred on by Hungerford's powerful rivals who hoped to benefit by the confiscation of estates that would inevitably follow once Agnes was found guilty of a capital crime.

The antiquarian William John Hardy, who uncovered many details of the case in the 1880s, says it does not follow that Hungerford necessarily knew about the murder. It seems unlikely, however, that he would not have had some inkling of what had gone on given that the murder had happened under his own roof and that at least one or several people in his household must have known about it already. After all, how else would such specific details of the murder come before the court within months of his death?

But just how did the case come before the courts with such detailed evidence of how Cotell had met his end? Somebody had been keeping the secret for four years and suddenly decided to bring it to light. This was a risky thing for anyone of humble origins to do when the accused was a member of the gentry. So who was it? The obvious candidate is her stepson Walter. He had the motive, having been seemingly left out of his father's will. Indeed, it was he who was to benefit from the king's confiscation of Agnes' possessions, for they would be returned to him by July that year. We know from his later behaviour towards Elizabeth Hungerford, that he had a ruthless streak. Perhaps it was he who denounced his 'wicked' stepmother, reckoning that she should get her just desserts for the crime.

Bolder theories might even be constructed. Is it possible that Agnes was a psychopathic social climber who killed not only Cotell but Edward too? That second death, so soon after the making of a will entirely drawn up in her favour, seems awfully convenient. Of course, another far-fetched idea could be proposed – that Walter had made up the murder of Cotell in order to get his hands on Farleigh Castle.

If Walter was playing a devious game he would eventually get his comeuppance. By 1540 he was out of favour, thought of harbouring sympathies with the Pilgrimage of Grace rebels. He was accused of treason, as well as witchcraft and buggery for good measure, and executed at Tower Hill on 28 July 1540. Alongside him facing execution was his former benefactor, Thomas Cromwell.

Elizabeth Hungerford survived her ordeals and went on to marry the courtier Sir Robert Throckmorton, with whom she had four children. She lived until 1554. Yet the curse on the relationships of the Hungerfords seems to have continued. Walter's heir, also called Walter, later tried to sue his wife, Anne, for divorce on the grounds that she had attempted to poison him and committed adultery. Having failed to prove the accusations he chose to be put in prison rather than support her financially. Wisely, she fled abroad.

Farleigh Hungerford Castle, near Bath, as it is today. It was the scene of John Cotell's murder in 1518. (Copyright James Moore)

Chapter 4

Butchered on the Bridge
1527

In Tudor England, committing murder was not always a hindrance to scaling the social ladder. And none advanced further after the calculated killing of a man than William Herbert, who went on to become the Earl of Pembroke and one of the richest men in the land. Herbert was nothing if not a survivor, arguably getting away with not just one murder but two, and then gaining the favour of four monarchs including Mary I, despite initially backing her opponent's bid for the throne.

Herbert's origins did not give much hint that he would eventually rise to become so powerful. His father, Sir Richard Herbert, from Ewyas, Herefordshire, was the illegitimate son of a former Earl of Pembroke, also called William Herbert. Known as Black William, the Earl had backed the Yorkist cause in the War of the Roses and been executed by the Lancastrians in 1469. His grandson, William, was one of perhaps as many as ten children, born in about 1506. As a younger son of one of the members of the lesser gentry, he does not seem to have had much of an education, remaining illiterate to his dying day. Even as a member of the Privy Council in the reign of Mary, he could only scrawl his initials in capital letters. The seventeenth century chronicler John Aubrey described Herbert as 'strong sett, but bony, reddish favoured, of a sharp eye' and 'stern look'. He also claims that he was a 'mad fighting young fellow' and relates that in his youth Herbert entered the service of a relative, the Earl of Worcester. Herbert was certainly a loose cannon and his hot-headed nature was soon to show itself.

On midsummer's eve 1527, there were a great number of Welshmen in the city of Bristol, or Bristowe as it was then known. One of these was William Herbert, then in his early twenties. No doubt drink was taken as midsummer was an important occasion for celebration in Tudor times marked by bonfires, marches and pageants. Things got out of hand and

A killing on the crossing. Bristol Bridge as it would have looked in the sixteenth century. (Copyright Look and Learn)

there was some kind of affray between the Welshmen and the watchmen, an incident serious enough to merit mention in the city's chronicles.

On 25 July, the mayor and some other city dignitaries were returning from watching a wrestling match in the city, a popular Tudor spectacle with wrestlers from the West Country considered the most skilled. The party then crossed Bristol Bridge, which spanned the River Avon and had given the city its name (Brycgstow meaning place of the bridge in Anglo-Saxon). At this time the bridge would have been lined with houses, just like London Bridge.

It was here that William Herbert, along with a group of young companions chose to confront them. It was a very public location and one from which it was difficult to escape, suggesting that some premeditation had gone into what was to follow.

Herbert's group was at least twenty strong, presumably outnumbering the older Bristolians. Among them were his step-brother, Thomas Bawdrip, also from Wales, Thomas Herbert from Mitchel Troy in Monmouthshire and another man with the same name who had also been in service of the Earl of Worcester. Joining this group was Walter Whitney, also of Mitchel Troy. These four 'gentlemen' were backed up by the yeomen David Williams from Chepstow and William Morgan from Cardiff along with a mariner named Lewis Ball and Walter Gurney, also from Chepstow and Cardiff respectively. There was one local man among them, John Herbert. Although he was living in Bristol it appears that he was originally from Wales too.

Whether William Herbert and his crew had the mercer William Vaughan in mind as a specific target, or just planned to cause trouble with some of the more important men in the town, we'll never know. Vaughan was an important man in the city and had been sheriff in 1516. He himself had a Welsh background – his family were originally from Cardigan. While there may have been some old issue of contention between him and the group of menacing men on the bridge, Bristol had a large Welsh population at the time and his roots were probably mere coincidence. It may have been that Vaughan simply tried to push past the rowdy young Welshmen, but Aubrey suggests that Herbert resisted arrest, perhaps for something that had happened on Midsummer Eve. Whatever the circumstances, offence was taken by Herbert and the others for 'want of some respect in complement' from Vaughan. The enraged Herbert, along with at least six of his accomplices, brandished their swords and Vaughan ended up suffering a bad wound on the right side of his head.

Leaving Vaughan in a pool of blood, the leading culprits then fled through the city gates and into the marshland that then surrounded much of the old city. They were heading for Lewis Ball's boat, which was waiting for them. A contemporary account suggests that Herbert and the others then set course for Wales and 'escaped cleare away in a boate with the tide without any hurt done to them'. On 2 August, Vaughan died from his injuries and what had been an assault now became a murder. An inquest was opened by the Bristol coroner and two days later the matter was brought before local magistrates. Herbert, in his absence, was indicted as one of the wanted men.

While the suspects for Vaughan's murder were long gone, his wife Joan was not about to let the matter lie. Realising that more muscle would be needed if they were ever going to be caught, she made an appeal to the court of the King's Bench at Westminster. The original coroner's report and indictment were brought before the King's Bench in October 1528 but nothing more seems to have been done to attempt to apprehend the culprits or give Joan any form of redress at this time.

Meanwhile, Herbert is thought to have fled to France. Aubrey says that 'he betooke himself into the army where he shewed so much courage, and readinesse of witt in conduct' that he came to the attention of the French king, Francis I, who is alleged to have written to Henry VIII highlighting his good conduct.

On 1 September, 1529, seemingly out of the blue, William Herbert along with both Thomas Herberts, as well as John Herbert were granted a royal pardon for Vaughan's death. The King's Bench was told to 'molest them no more' and on 28 October, now back in England, they presented themselves before the court where the case against them was dismissed. It is probable that the Herberts had agreed to pay Joan some compensation for the death of her husband. Official records show that the 'parties were agreed'.

Why Henry should favour a relatively lowly fellow like Herbert in such a case is a puzzle. Perhaps it was simply because Herbert's family had served his own well. Herbert's father had been a gentleman usher to Henry VII and had apparently been knighted by Henry VIII towards the end of his life. There's evidence that some of the others involved in Vaughan's killing, including Thomas Bawdrip and William Morgan, were not pardoned and proceedings continued against them. Herbert, however, soon got a job in service to the king.

Four years after his rampage in Bristol, Herbert's quick-tempered nature caused him to come to the attention of the courts once again. In 1531, he was brought up, along with his brother George, and two other men including his servant Richard Lewis, over a fatal assault carried out in London. Again the victim was a Welshman, Richard ap Ieuan ap Jenkyn. Sadly, further details of the case are scant, but if Jenkyn's death was the result of another dust up in the street it is likely that Herbert claimed self-defence and that his royal connections meant that, once again, he got away with it.

Ironically it was his very fighting abilities that Henry probably valued in Herbert. Indeed, tradition has it that the king was impressed by Herbert's sword fighting skills when he once observed him showing off outside Whitehall Palace. Herbert must have had some charm too; at court he met Anne Parr and the couple were married in 1538. Anne was a woman much better educated than Herbert and it seems an unlikely match, but in an era when it was easy to lose one's head by choosing the wrong faction, Anne shared a common trait with Herbert. She was also a survivor and in fact both William and Anne continued to retain royal favour throughout their lives. Anne, described as 'a most faithful wife, a woman of the greatest piety and discretion' had the unusual distinction of acting as lady-in-waiting to all of the king's six wives – no mean feat.

Herbert's success at court soon brought him riches and in the early 1540s he acquired the lands belonging to Wilton Abbey in Wiltshire where he set up home, building a grand house. His positon was strengthened further when Henry married Anne's sister, Catherine Parr in 1543. Herbert, know knighted, was also distinguishing himself on the battlefield fighting for Henry in France during the campaign of 1544. He became keeper of Baynard's Castle in London and owner of Cardiff Castle too. Under Edward VI his influence grew as he helped put down a rebellion in the West Country and he became a privy councillor. More land came his way and he was made the Earl of Pembroke in 1551.

Herbert's fortunes might have faltered after he married off his eldest son Henry to Lady Catherine Grey, the sister of Lady Jane Grey. When Lady Jane briefly found herself on the throne Pembroke, inclined to Protestantism, initially appeared to back her claim to the English crown. But he was ever the tactician and when Mary gained the upper hand in her bid to be queen he switched sides, throwing Lady Catherine out of his house and getting the marriage between her and Henry annulled. Despite his political manoeuvring, Pembroke's taste for a bit of action had not deserted him in later life as he vowed that, 'eyther this sword shall make Mary Quene, or Ile lose my life.'

He was soon to prove his worth to the new regime by helping to quash Wyatt's rebellion which briefly threatened the capital in 1554 and was still leading troops for Mary's army in 1557. He continued serving on the Privy Council into Elizabeth I's reign. Somewhat surprisingly, the Earl died in his bed, at Hampton Court, in 1570 and was buried in St Paul's Cathedral.

Chapter 5

A Cook who was Boiled Alive
1531

'This yere was a coke boylyd in a cauderne in Smythfeld for he wolde a powsyned the bishop of Rochester Fycher with dyvers of hys servanttes, and he was lockyd in a chayne and pullyd up and downe with a gybbyt at dyvers tymes tyll he was dede.'

This was how the *Chronicle of the Grey Friars of London* reported the demise of Richard Roose, a man from humble origins who met an excruciating end, his ghastly punishment deemed appropriate for perpetrating one of the most devious and wicked crimes of his time. Yet the manner of Roose's execution becomes all the more distressing once one delves into the murky background to the case which has since emerged from the shadows of history. For it seems that this humble cook may well have been an unwitting dupe in a plot to kill his employer and an unfortunate victim of the simmering political tensions of the age.

Roose, also known as Richard Coke, worked in the kitchens of John Fisher, the Bishop of Rochester, who was one of the foremost ecclesiastical figures of his day. Like the better known Sir Thomas More and Cardinal Wolsey, Fisher had for many years enjoyed royal favour and patronage. The son of a Yorkshire merchant, he was educated at the University of Cambridge and eventually became its chancellor. His talents caught the eye of Henry VII who, in 1504, made him Bishop of Rochester while still in his thirties. Fisher also acted as personal chaplain to Margaret Beaufort, Henry's mother and he was chosen to give the funeral oration at Henry's funeral in 1509. He helped tutor Henry VIII and was considered one of the finest theologians of his day. The scholar Erasmus lauded him as, 'the one man at this time who is incomparable for uprightness of life, for learning and for greatness of soul.' Despite his abilities Fisher possessed a rather dour nature; this was a man who kept a skull on his table at mealtimes to remind him of imminent death. It was as if he had a presentiment of what was to come.

In the early part of Henry VIII's reign, Fisher was an important ally of the king. Henry boasted that he was glad to be able to rely on such 'a learned man, such a good man' as Fisher. But when Henry began his attempts to divorce his first wife, Catherine of Aragon, it put the pair at loggerheads. Fisher became one of the most vehement supporters of her cause, going on to write as many as eight books in defence of her marriage to Henry.

By the early 1530s, Fisher was briefly imprisoned for resisting Henry's attempts to limit the power of the clergy. Once released, he continued to oppose the king's bid to be recognised as head of the English church. By 1531, it appears that Fisher was, in many ways, already a marked man whose enemies were circling, looking for any opportunity to bring him down. Indeed, Henry let it be known that the bishop and his adherents should be 'thrown into the river' if they did not fall in line with his will.

On 18 February that year, a large broth or gruel was made in the kitchens of the Bishop's residence in Lambeth Marsh. It was designed to be eaten by all of those in the household, including members of Fisher's family. In the hours that followed, as many as sixteen or seventeen of the diners became very unwell. One gentleman, Benett Curwen, died in agony. Some of the beggars who congregated near the house hoping to benefit from the leftovers which were habitually handed out as charity, were 'lyke wyse infected' after eating some of the pottage. One of them, a widow called Alyce Tryppytt, also perished. It was assumed that those who had suffered had been the victims of an intentional poisoning plot.

One man who hadn't been affected was 62-year-old Bishop Fisher. Stow tells us that he 'eate no pottage that day.' Another account says that Fisher, described elsewhere as being in poor health at this period, announced he had no appetite that dinner time and said he would eat later in the evening. But rumour was rife that he had been the real target and the scandal rocked London. Poisoning engendered huge fear in the Tudor elite and the matter came to the direct attention of the king. He abhorred 'such abhomynable offences'. Using such a device to murder meant that no one could 'lyve in suertye out of daunger of death'.

A culprit was duly found. Roose was dragged out of the kitchens and arrested. An obscure record in the Venetian archives states that under interrogation on the rack the cook confessed that he had indeed added a nameless powder to the meal, but said that it had all been meant as a 'jest'. He had thought the offending substance merely a laxative. Eustace Chapuys, Charles V's ambassador to England, wrote in a letter to his master at the time that, 'The cook was immediately seized, at the instance of the bishop's brother, and, it is said, confessed he had thrown in a powder which, he had been given to understand, would only hocus the servants, without doing them any harm.' Nevertheless the king felt that his crime was so outrageous that Roose should not be put on trial for murder in the usual way. To the surprise of many he was, instead, arraigned for high treason as if he had made an attempt to murder one of the royal family themselves. Indeed, on 28 February, Henry appeared at the House of Lords himself and spoke for an hour and a half on the subject of poisoning.

So heinous was the crime, according to the king, that this 'detestable offence nowe newly practysed and comytted requyreth condygne punysshemente for the same'. A special law was quickly introduced by parliament allowing Roose, and anyone else found guilty of the crime, to be boiled to death. The statute, known as the Acte for Poysoning, mentioned Roose specifically, describing him as a man of a 'moste wyked and dampnable dysposicyon' who had cast a 'certyne venym or poyson into a vessell replenysshed with yeste or barme stondyng in the kechyn.' This had been used to make the broth.

The act 'ordeyned and enacted … that the said Richard Roose shalbe therfore boyled to deathe.' He would not, the act pointed out, be allowed benefit of clergy (see page 14). No jury would sit in judgement. The verdict had been summarily reached.

On 5 April, Roose was brought to Smithfield where he was lowered several times into the vat of boiling water on a chain until he was slowly scalded to death. One chronicler described the full horror of Roose's ordeal - 'He roared mighty loud and divers women who were big with child did feel sick at the sight of what they saw, and were carried away half dead; and other men and women did not seem frightened by the boiling alive, but would prefer to see the headsman at his work.'

Even at the time many doubted that Roose had acted alone. Given how seriously poisoning was viewed even before the new, desperate punishment that had been enacted by Henry, would Roose really have taken the risk of putting something toxic into the soup simply for fun? It's much more likely that he was encouraged to do so by someone of a higher social standing and simply did what he was told without knowing what the substance was or considering the consequences for himself or Bishop Fisher.

The unprecedented personal intervention in the affair, as well as the extreme punishment he had deemed necessary for the crime, led some to think that the king protested too much. There were whispers that it was all a smokescreen for the fact he himself was involved in a plot to murder Fisher in retaliation for the latter's obstructive behaviour over Henry's divorce. Chapuys wrote of Roose, 'I do not yet know whom he has accused of giving him this powder, nor the issue of the affair. The king has done well to show dissatisfaction at this; nevertheless, he cannot wholly avoid some suspicion, if not against himself, whom I think too good to do such a thing, at least against the lady and her father.'

This astute foreign diplomat's assessment was probably accurate. It is unlikely that Henry would use such a method to rid himself of the troublesome priest. There is no doubt that Henry would rather have had Fisher out of the way, but his technique of exterminating enemies was far more nuanced, as would be shown in the following years. It is even possible to take his own views on poisoning at face value, fearing that his enemies would use this method to assassinate him and making an example of Roose to warn off anyone who might consider it.

As it in fact transpired, a blanket poisoning was a very inefficient way of ensuring a particular person's death and Henry's agents might have been able to come up with a more foolproof method of killing Fisher. So was it just a prank gone wrong or did someone else have a grievance against Fisher? Were they perhaps not so much trying to kill Fisher himself but deliver a chilling warning of the fate that awaited him if he continued to oppose their interests? The obvious suspects in this scenario, as Chapuys hints, are Anne Boleyn and her father, the Earl of Wiltshire, who saw Fisher as one of the leading and most vocal opponents to their advancement at court.

Rumours to this effect were certainly doing the rounds at the time and were fuelled by a another strange incident after the murder attempt, when a cannonball was fired across the Thames into the roof of the Bishop's house, narrowly missing him while he sat in his study. The shot was alleged to have come from the Earl of Wiltshire's house, though there seems to be no explanation of whether this was deemed an accident or an intentional act at the time. Certainly, Fisher concluded that his life was in peril and left London for Rochester. In October 1531, Anne Boleyn sent a message to Fisher warning him not to attend the next session of Parliament. She was, she said, concerned that he should not get sick again as he had been in the February. It was only a very thinly veiled threat. At the same time Chapuys wrote that, 'There is no one here of whom the Lady is more afraid than the Bishop of Rochester …'

Given the campaign of intimidation against him it was unsurprising that Fisher was now in poor health, though he was, it seems, secretly intriguing against the king with Charles V through Chapuys. In 1534, Fisher was briefly imprisoned for supposedly not reporting all the revelations of the Maid of Kent, Elizabeth Barton. And when, in April, he refused to take the oath of succession thereby acknowledging that the issue of Henry and his new wife Anne were legitimate heirs to the throne, he was thrown in the Tower of London where he languished in severe conditions for more than a year. Stripped of his title and goods he was tricked into openly admitting that he did not see the king as supreme head of the Church and, despite being made a Cardinal by Pope Paul III while still behind bars, Fisher was tried for treason as a commoner.

On 17 June, at Westminster, Fisher was found guilty and originally sentenced to be hanged, drawn and quartered at Tyburn. The king was only merciful in as much as this was commuted to beheading, largely due to public disquiet. On 22 June 1535, Fisher appeared before the crowd at Tower Hill, an emaciated and defeated figure. Decapitated in front of them, his body was then left naked on the scaffold until evening, while his head was stuck on a pole on London Bridge.

Fisher's death was undoubtedly less painful than being poisoned, or being boiled to death like Roose for that matter. Nevertheless it was a sad and humiliating end for a man who had once been held in such esteem. Fisher's death was to herald a wave of executions of high profile figures in the following few years. If Anne Boleyn had been behind the murder attempt on Fisher's life it didn't help her live much longer. Having become a nuisance to Henry, she went to the chopping block less than a year later. Like Sir Thomas More, who was put to death in July 1535, Fisher was later beatified by the Pope. Roose, the man who had suffered gruesomely for, at worst, being a hapless accessory to murder, became merely another bloody footnote in the annals of Henry's reign of terror.

Chapter 6

Gunned Down in the Morning Mist 1536

On the chill morning of Monday 13 November, 1536, a heavy mist hung in the streets of London. At 5am there were few others stirring as the wealthy merchant Robert Packyngton stepped out of his home on Cheapside making for the thirteenth century church of St Thomas of Acre where he was planning to attend mass. This was a ritual he was known to carry out every day without fail.

Suddenly, there was a loud bang. Many of Robert's neighbours heard the noise, along with some labourers already at work in nearby Soper Lane, some of whom had seen this 'man of good substaunce' emerge from his home. Not many would have recognised the thunderous clap as the noise of a gun going off but, at the sound, Robert was seen to slump to the ground. He had been shot dead.

Murders committed using firearms were almost unknown in early Tudor England. In fact this may have been the capital's first. So Packyngton's demise was one that would shock the nation. Yet, as the sixteenth century Chronicler Edward Hall put it, the 'deed-doer' was 'unespied and unknown'. Perhaps the gunman had used the mist as a cover for his crime. Indeed the method of murder suggested a cunning, well planned assassination.

Robert Packyngton was born in 1489 in Stanford-on-Teme, Worcestershire, into a family of landowners. His older brother, Sir John Packyngton became a successful lawyer. Robert first trained as a lawyer too but, by 1510, had completed his apprenticeship in the Mercer's Company and began work as a merchant exporting cloth and importing 'sundry wares.'

By the time of his death Packyngton was primarily an exporter of cloth who frequently travelled to the Netherlands on business. In 1535, he is known to have exported a total of 250 cloths to Antwerp. He had also represented the Mercers' interests as a Member of Parliament, speaking 'somewhat against the covetousness and crueltie of the clergie'. He sat in the parliament of 1529 that would oversee the Reformation and was later described as a man who brought 'English bybles from beyond the sea' indicating that he sympathized with the religious revolution beginning to sweep England. Indeed, his brother Augustine is recorded as having tricked Cuthbert Tunstall, the Bishop London, into thinking he had bought all of William Tyndale's remaining English bibles from the Low Countries so that he could burn them at St Paul's. Augustine gave Tyndale the money and then he simply printed a new version.

From the archives, it emerges that in the months before Packyngton's death – thanks to his travels to the Netherlands on business – he had been reporting to Henry's right hand man, Thomas Cromwell. Stephen Vaughan, one of Cromwell's spies, thought him important enough to advise his master to 'cherisshe him and geve hym thankes.' It's not known what kind of information Packyngton was passing to Cromwell, but it certainly made him a player in the tumultuous politics of the 1530s and could have made him enemies. Indeed, he seems to have been well aware of the risks, making an early will a year before his death, carefully providing for his 'lytell' children.

Packyngton was buried in St Pancras church but after his murder the mystery about who had perpetrated it quickly grew, becoming a talking point across the land. However, despite a proclamation by the mayor of London that there would be a 'gret rewarde' for any information that could help identify his killer, none was forthcoming. In the coming years most of the suspicion fell upon the clergy, by this time a popular target. The Protestant reformer John Bale suggested that 'conservative bishops' were behind the slaying, while the lawyer and chronicler Edward Hall also thought that the established clergy must be to blame saying, 'he was had in contempt with theim, and therefore mooste lyke by one of theim thus shamefully murdered.'

It was left to another prominent historian, John Foxe, in the late 1550s, to name an actual person in relation to Packyngton's murder. He accused John Stokesley, the Bishop of London at the time, asserting that he had paid a priest the sum of sixty gold coins to perpetrate the deed. Later, Foxe changed his story, asserting that it was the Dean of St. Paul's, John Incent, who ordered the murder and who had confessed as much on his deathbed. Foxe intimated that a shady Italian had been hired to carry out

Portrait of Thomas Cromwell, advisor to King Henry VIII. (Courtesy Wellcome Library, London)

the shooting. Most of those who wrote accounts of Packyngton's murder did so from a Protestant point of view, but could provide little evidence of a detailed conspiracy by the Church. Indeed, John Incent was one of Cromwell's closest allies. Incidentally, Foxe also reported that at the time of Packyngton's murder there were rumours that Robert Singleton, a one-time chaplain to Anne Boleyn, was being talked of as being the murderer, but he dismisses the idea. Singleton is known to have been an agent of Cromwell and was put to death in 1544 for treason.

There is no doubt that Packyngton sympathised with Lutheran thinking and, at his funeral on 16 November, the sermon was read by the leading Protestant reformer Robert Barnes. But the later conflicting accounts of Packyngton's demise from those who supported Henry's purge of the old order and their difficulty on agreeing on a single named culprit are unconvicing. It seems outlandish for the Church to have gone to such lengths to kill one individual who was known to be anti-clerical. There were many others who, like Packyngton, posed a threat but were not murdered in the same way.

By the time that Holinshed's famous *Chronicles* were published in the 1570s, proponents of the old religion were no longer in the frame. He recorded that the real murderer was a much more humble soul who had been caught for another crime at Banbury in Oxfordshire. Condemned to death, the unnamed man was brought to the gallows where, apparently, he suddenly confessed to Packyngton's murder. It is likely that this story can be discounted as criminals making wild boasts from the gallows were quite common in a time when a public hanging was something of an entertainment and this version of events only emerges in the records some forty years after the murder.

Holinshed's tale also appears unsatisfactory when the manner of Packyngton's death is considered. It has all the hallmarks of a professional hitman equipped with the latest weapon and with the cunning to make his escape unseen. Foxe's suggestion that a foreigner was to blame may hold some weight. Whoever did kill Packyngton, this was unlikely to have been the work of one man acting alone but part of a wider plot. Those who wanted Packyngton done away with clearly wanted him dead very badly and knew how to cover their tracks. What did he know? What risk did he pose? We can be pretty sure that he was involved in espionage on some level and was linked with Cromwell, a slippery character.

One intriguing theory is that it was all a case of mistaken identity and that Packyngton's death was organised by allies of Tunstall who were actually meant to kill his brother, Augustine, for that embarrassing ruse regarding the bibles. The problem with this idea is that Augustine was already dead and that what we know about Tunstall's politically meek character makes him an unlikely candidate for such intrigue in any case.

Another possibility is that his murder was nothing to do with the religious turmoil going on in England at the time. There is a tendency to see any dramatic incident during these years as somehow connected to the Reformation. Could it just as easily have been the result of a business transaction that had gone wrong, perhaps on the continent and for which retribution was being exacted? Of course this is mere speculation and the Packyngton murder remains a perplexing 'whodunit' to this day.

Chapter 7

A Posh Poacher Snared in the Noose 1541

Thomas Fiennes, 9th Baron Dacre, made something of a habit of sending people to their deaths. In 1536, he had been present as one of the members of the jury at the trial of Anne Boleyn, Henry VIII's second wife, on charges of adultery, incest and treason. Along with twenty-six other hand-picked 'yes men' he duly found the queen guilty and she was beheaded at the Tower of London on 19 May. Following the failed Pilgrimage of Grace, a northern uprising against Henry in the autumn of 1536, Dacre was again one of those trusted enough by the king to sit on a jury to condemn the rebel lords Darcy and Hussey to die. Again, in 1538, Dacre's services were required to try the Marquess of Exeter for a rebellion in the West Country; Exeter went to the block later that year.

Like many of the men who played a part in condemning those who had incurred the king's wrath during that dangerous era, Dacre must have occasionally wondered whether he might, one day, suffer a similar fate. After all, more nobles would be executed during Henry VIII's reign than under any other monarch. Yet it is unlikely that Dacre ever imagined that a mere midnight jolly would see him locked up in the tower facing the ultimate penalty. For it was not high treason or political power games that would see him come a cropper, but a case of youthful high jinks leading to hapless murder.

Fiennes succeeded to his title in 1533 aged about seventeen. The family seat was the grand, fifteenth century brick-built Herstmonceux Castle in Sussex and Dacre owned property worth £1200 a year – a fortune at the time. In 1534, he was summoned to attend parliament and quickly became well known at court. Over the next few years, he established himself as one of Henry's favourites, attending the christening of the future Edward VI. In 1537, he was chosen to help carry the canopy at the funeral of Jane Seymour, Henry's third wife, when she died in

October 1537. Dacre was also in a party that received Anne of Cleves in Rainham, Kent when Henry's prospective new wife arrived in England in 1540.

Dacre may have been rubbing shoulders with the most important folk in the land and a married man, but he was still a typical twenty-something, prone to get involved in the odd caper. In 1537, his youthful antics got him into trouble with the second most important man in England, Thomas Cromwell. He had been forced to write an apologetic letter to Henry's right-hand man: 'I have received your lordship's letters wherin I perceive your benevolence towards the frailness of my youth in considering that I was rather led by instigation of my accusers than of my mere mind of those unlawful acts, which I have long detested in secret. I perceive your lordship is desirous to have knowledge of all riotous hunters and shall exert myself to do you service therin.'

We don't know the back story of the incident to which Dacre refers, but, given the fate that later befell him, its contents are extremely telling. The peer obviously had a penchant for prank poaching with his aristocratic pals. In 1541 one of these perilous late night escapades would end in disaster.

On 20 April, Dacre and thirteen of his associates met at Herstmonceux to conspire to hunt on the lands of Nicholas Pelham, another important Sussex landowner who owned the neighbouring estate at Laughton. They planned to take dogs and large nets with them to catch deer. According to a later hearing of local JPs, the 26-year old and his associates had then 'bound themselves by oaths' to kill anyone who might oppose them. On the night of 30 April they met again and divided into two groups, setting off for different parts of Pelham's estate. According to Holinshed, Dacre's group consisted of John Mauntell, John Frowdys, George Roydon, John Cheyne, Thomas Isley, Richard Middleton and John Goldwell. They went to a plot of land called Pykhaye in the parish of Hellingly. There they came across John Busebrygge, James Busebrygge and Richard Sumner, evidently some of Pelham's employees and, fearing that they might be recognised by the trio, attacked them. Holinshed says: 'there insued a fraie betwixt the said lord Dacres and his companie on the one partie, and the said John and James Busebrygge and Richard Sumner on the other.' According to the coroner's report the incident occurred between 8-10pm.

John Busebrygge ended up with a wound on the left side of his back though it's not clear who inflicted the blow. Carried back to Pelham's house, Laughton Place, he died from his injuries two days later. Dacre and his seven companions had fled the scene of the attack, but Pelham's men had, indeed, recognised and reported them.

No doubt Dacre's adventure was all meant to be a great wheeze, but it had gone tragically wrong and the authorities took a dim view. Deer stealing itself was a serious crime, but killing another gentleman's servant in the process meant the local justices of the peace got involved. Dacre was taken into custody and imprisoned in the Tower of London. He was due to face a charge of murder at the Palace of Westminster but there was heated debate among the members of the Privy Council in the Star Chamber about the case. On 27 June, Sir William Paget, clerk to the Council, wrote that he had heard the lords arguing about whether, legally, this really was a case of wilful murder, as Dacre had not planned to kill Busebrygge. But they eventually agreed that his plea should be heard.

Dacre at first pleaded not guilty 'declaring, with long circumstances that he intended no murder' but he was subsequently persuaded to change this plea at the encouragement of some of some peers on the basis that some of the other men accused along with him had already confessed. Reluctantly, Dacre now refused his trial hoping to throw himself on the king's mercy. The council meanwhile asked the king to pardon their fellow aristocrat. Earlier in Henry's life this ploy might have worked. But by the 1540s Henry was growing ever more spiteful; he point blank refused and Dacre was promptly sentenced to death.

There was more humiliation to come. Dacre was scheduled to be beheaded on 29 June. But on the morning of his execution, as he was brought out of the Tower, a messenger suddenly arrived with a stay of execution. Dacre must have thought that finally he was to get a reprieve from the king. It was a cruel trick. In fact he was not to suffer the death of a noble, but of a common criminal – hanged at Tyburn. His end was merely delayed by a few hours. Holinshed tells us, 'at three of the clocke in the same afternoon, he was brought forth of the tower and delivered to the sherrifs who led him on foote betwixt them unto Tiburne where he died.' Edward Hall described how Dacre 'was strangled as common murderers are and his body buried in the church of St Sepulchre.' The diplomat Eustace Chapuys, wrote that Dacre 'was hung from the most ignominious gibbet, and for the greater shame dragged through the streets to the place of execution, to the great pity of many people.'

So what of the rest of Dacre's party? Mauntell, Frowdys and Roydon had all been brought to the court of the King's Bench as well and been persuaded that it was in their best interests to plead guilty. It wasn't. They were hanged on the same day as Dacre, but at another traditional place of execution, St Thomas-a-Watering, where the River Neckinger crossed the main route leading south east out of the city. Demonstrating Henry's inconsistency during this period, Cheyne somehow managed to secure himself an early pardon while Goldwell, Isley and Middleton were pardoned later, in 1542, despite initially having been sentenced to death. The men in the second group who had been poaching that night merely faced fines.

Dacre's family were stripped of titles and lands but financial provision was made for his wife Mary who married again and lived another thirty-five years. On the accession of Elizabeth, Dacre's title and lands were restored to his son Gregory, who became the 10th Baron Dacre. Dacre's daughter Margaret later became Baroness Dacre. She married an MP, had eleven children and set up home at Herstmonceux once again.

Chapter 8

Stabbed and Dangled From a Castle Window 1546

On 28 May 1546, Cardinal David Beaton enjoyed an intimate night with his mistress, Marion Ogilvy, at his home – the impressive St Andrews Castle in Fife on the Eastern coast of Scotland. It was to be the lovers' last night of passion. At five o'clock in the morning, Ogilvy left by the postern gate. Watching her leave were a group of around sixteen secret assassins and by the end of the morning the Cardinal would have suffered an horrific death at their hands.

Like many bloody killings in the sixteenth century, the story of Beaton's murder had its roots in the religious ferment of the era, as the leaders of the Catholic Church tussled with those bent on reform. But it was also a product of the tempestuous swirl of Scottish politics as rival factions jostled for supremacy. After Henry VIII's split with Rome in the 1530s the English monarch was keen to exert greater influence over Scotland. In the early 1540s the king of Scotland was James V, the son of Margaret Tudor, daughter of Henry VII and so the nephew of Henry VIII. However, James showed little interest in moving closer to the English instead pursuing a policy of closer ties with France. Indeed, Beaton had been instrumental in arranging James' marriages to two French aristocrats, first Madeleine of Valois and then Mary of Guise. James died soon after Henry's forces invaded and defeated the Scots at the Battle of Solway Moss in November 1542. His heir, Mary, who would one day rule as Mary Queen of Scots, was just a few days old and too young to take charge. For a time, a new pro-Protestant regent, James Hamilton, the 2nd Earl of Arran, took the reins of power and looked to form stronger links with England. Beaton's ploy to seize power using a faked will from the late king was foiled and he was

The murder of Cardinal Beaton. Illustration from *The People's History of England, 1890.* (Copyright Look and Learn)

initially imprisoned, while Arran agreed a treaty with Henry that set out a future marriage between his son, Prince Edward (the future Edward VI) and Mary.

However, the wily Beaton soon wriggled free from captivity and established the upper hand in his struggle with Arran, convincing enough Scottish nobles and church men that their interests lay in supporting his Catholic, pro-French outlook. Eventually Arran fell in line, with the hope that his own son, James, might one day marry Mary. The prospect of a union with England began to recede.

Beaton's personal life seemed to make a nonsense of his vows of celibacy as an ordained member of the clergy. For years he conducted a relationship with Ogilvy and fathered eight children by her. The couple lived openly together for some time. Beaton's own laxity when it came to Church rules didn't stop him pursuing the persecution of those who wanted to reform it. The action which caused the greatest disquiet was when he ordered the arrest of the mild mannered Protestant preacher George Wishart in December 1545. Wishart was promptly thrown into the infamous Bottle Dungeon, below the Sea Tower at St Andrews Castle, awaiting trial. Named after its shape, this dank dungeon was dug out of the bare rock and could only be accessed by a small hole using a rope or ladder. Found guilty of heresy, Wishart was burned to death outside the castle walls on 1 March, 1546.

Such extremism made Beaton unpopular, though it seems that the conspirators who now planned the Cardinal's murder were driven as much by personal animosities than outrage over Wishart's callous killing or reformist religious zeal. There were also promises of advancement from the English if Beaton, who remained an obstacle to Henry's expansionist plans, was removed. Leading the plotters was the Master of Rothes, Norman Leslie, a nobleman who had recently fallen out with Beaton, probably over property. He was joined by a string of other members of the Scottish gentry including his uncle, John Leslie of Parkhill, James Melville of Carnbee, William Kirkcaldy of Grange and Peter Carmichael of Balmedie.

That sultry May, with English attacks an ever-present threat, Beaton had been spending large sums on refortifying St Andrews Castle. By the early hours of 29th there were scores of people already bringing in lime and stone to the fortress. Knowing that the work was going on and that the drawbridge would be lowered to let workers in, Beaton's attackers had gathered in the nearby abbey church yard, disguised as stonemasons. At six o'clock they made to enter the castle via the drawbridge. Kirkcaldy began to engage the porter, Ambrose Stirling, in conversation asking whether the Cardinal was yet awake, while Norman Leslie and others managed to slip in unnoticed. But Stirling became suspicious when he saw John Leslie and some others entering 'somewhat roughly' and tried to close the drawbridge. He was immediately set upon by Leslie who hit the gatekeeper over the head, grabbed his keys and threw his dead body in the moat.

Norman Leslie, at least, knew the layout of the castle but the relative ease of the gang's entry suggests that some of the members of the hundred-strong garrison were in on the plot. In any case, the remaining workers and members of the garrison were quickly ejected and no-one else was hurt as the attackers took control. The castle gates were locked and some of the party went in search of Beaton, now alone with his valet somewhere inside. By this time, Beaton had got wind of what was going on. He attempted to flee via the postern gate but saw it was guarded by Kirkcaldy. He decided to shut himself in his personal chamber and, together with his servant, 'put chests and other barriers' against the door as a barricade.

The main account of what happened next comes down to us via John Knox, the famous Protestant reformer who later entered the castle in support of the assassins. Knox got his information from the murderers themselves and tells us that when three of the attackers, John Leslie, Peter Carmichael and James Melville, arrived at Beaton's door they found it locked and tried to break it down. From inside, the Cardinal began trying to bargain with them asking to see Norman, who he described as 'his friend'. The attackers ignored him and and started a fire at the foot of the door. Knowing he was trapped Beaton now ordered it to be opened, evidently hoping to talk his way out of the situation. He slumped into a chair and begged the trio to remember that he was a member of the clergy, crying, 'I ame a priest, I ame a priest, ye wil not slay me.'

His desperate pleas did him no good. John Leslie immediately stepped forward and stabbed him, then Carmichael drew his blade and did the same. It fell to the usually 'gentle' and 'modest' James Melville, a close friend of the dead Wishart, to deliver the fatal blows. He said, 'This work and judgment of God ought to be done with greater gravity' and launched into a speech directed against Beaton telling the prone prelate to 'repent of thy former wickit lyif' before plunging his sword into his body two or three times. The Cardinal died, crying, 'Fie, fie all is gone.'

The news of the attack on the castle spread like wildfire throughout the town and soon a crowd had gathered, demanding to see the Cardinal. To prove that he was already dead and the matter settled, the killers tied some sheets together, attached them to Beaton's lifeless body by the leg and arm and unceremoniously slung the corpse out of a window down the side of the castle wall. The chronicler Robert Lindsay of Pitscottie recounted how, at this moment, a man called Guthrie, possibly the Cardinal's own page, stepped forward, undid his clothes and 'pischit' in the Cardinal's mouth that, 'all the pepill might sie,' crowning Beaton's humiliation.

Beaton's corpse was salted and put in a lead coffin. Then, in a sort of poetic justice for what had happened to Wishart, he was thrown in the Bottle Dungeon where the body was kept for more than nine months before finally being buried, without great ceremony, at the convent of the Blackfriars at St. Andrews.

The murderers, dubbed the Castilians, took control of the castle and a stalemate ensued, partly because they had taken the Earl of Arran's son as a hostage. As the stand-off continued, the possibility of a Papal pardon was even raised. Meanwhile the defenders gained more supporters, such as Knox, and drew supplies from the surrounding countryside, indulging in a spot of 'leichorie with fair wemen,' as they did so. By the new year, Henry VIII had died and with the new English lord protector, the Duke of Somerset, sending only limited support to the defenders, they faced a prolonged siege, finally realising that the game was up when a French fleet arrived and large guns were trained on the castle. The force capitulated on 30 July and those responsible for Beaton's death were taken prisoner aboard the French ships. John Knox was put to work as a galley slave.

None of those responsible for Beaton's murder would, however, be executed for their crime. James Melville died a natural death in captivity at the Castle of Brest in Brittany. But by 1550, all of the Castilians still surviving had been freed. Norman Leslie ended up serving as a soldier for the French King Henry II and died in battle, at Renti, in 1554. Kirkcaldy would go on to work as a spy for the English. His sentence for murder was lifted in 1556 during a period of rapprochement and he eventually returned to Scotland, though he was later hanged, in 1573, after backing the imprisoned Queen Mary. John Leslie was restored to his lands in 1575, forgiven by the Cardinal's 'friends' and survived until 1585. Meanwhile, Knox became royal chaplain to Edward VI and subsequently helped continue the Protestant revolution in Scotland which, partly due to the death of Beaton, gained ascendancy. This must have left Beaton turning in his grave. Indeed his troubled spirit has been felt at Ethie Castle near Arbroath, a home he once shared with Marion Ogilvy. The strange thumping sounds to be heard at night are put down to the Cardinal dragging his gout ridden leg behind him as his spectre stalks the corridors.

Chapter 9

Butchered During a Game of Backgammon 1551

There is a half-timbered house that stands on the corner of Abbey Street and Abbey Place in Faversham, Kent, which at first glance appears to be just another fine example of the many impressive historic buildings that line the ancient thoroughfares of this small town. Yet this higgledy-piggledy property, which dates back more than 500 years, is somewhat taller than the others nearby and retains a melancholy air even on a sunny day; its upper storeys leaning out menacingly over the road below. The sullen appearance of what is known today as 'Arden House' takes on a more chilling dimension when you take a closer look at its street-side wall where there is a small plaque. It recalls the location's dark and infamous past, revealing why the building has deserved special attention in the annals of this humble market town. For it was within these very walls that the house's former owner, one Thomas Arden, was gruesomely murdered on the evening of 15 February, 1551.

Given its sordid nature, the Arden case sent shockwaves through the nation at the time. Indeed, the spellbinding story surrounding Arden's death was still proving gripping decades later when the celebrated play *Arden of Faversham*, was written based upon this real-life thriller, possibly by William Shakespeare himself. The case would continue to be a subject of fascination for balladeers, playwrights and historians for centuries to come.

The true story which provided the plot for *Arden of Faversham* did not need much elaboration for dramatic purposes. The play's main elements were very much based on cold, hard facts. And the real-life cast list might have been made for the stage. Indeed Raphael Holinshed found the Arden story so enticing that he gave it special attention in his famous

The murder of Thomas Arden in 1551, from a woodcut in the 1592 edition of the play *Arden of Faversham*. (Copyright Look and Learn/Peter Jackson Collection)

Chronicles, a tome in which other murders of 'ordinary' folk are sometimes mentioned, but rarely dwelt upon. Yet of the Arden case he said, 'The which murder, for the horribleness thereof … I have thought good to set it forth somewhat at large …'

By the time Thomas Arden met his end he was a successful and wealthy man. He was of a 'tall and comely personage' and may, originally, have been from Norwich, where it is thought he was born in 1508 into a family with a mercantile background. However, his later riches were built up following the dissolution of the monasteries under Henry VIII. In the 1530s, Arden was a clerk working on transactions involving monastic property. He was in the employment of Sir Edward North, who would later become Chancellor of the Augmentations, in charge of redistributing confiscated church lands. Arden also worked for Sir Thomas Cheyne, who was Warden of the Cinque Ports and probably thanks to his influence he would go on to become a successful local customs official. Arden also used his knowledge and connections to snap up lands belonging to the former Benedictine abbey in Faversham. These included today's Arden House, which had originally been the abbey's guest-house and, in the sixteenth century, would have stood next to the abbey's complex's outer gateway. By the 1540s, Arden was an important player among the leading men of Faversham. He became an alderman and, in 1548, for a short time the town's mayor.

In about 1537, Arden married a younger woman, Alice Brigandine, the daughter of a navy captain, who had become Sir Edward North's stepdaughter. According to Holinshed, Alice was, 'tall and well favoured of shape and countenance.' The Faversham historian Patricia Hyde has put the age difference between Arden and Alice at about thirteen years, reckoning that Arden was about forty-three at the time of his death and Alice was roughly thirty. The couple may also have had a daughter together called Margaret.

At some point, the discontented Alice fell for the charms of a tailor and servant of Sir Edward North, called Thomas Morsby, a much younger man than her spouse. Alice and Morsby began an affair. At one point their relationship faltered but Alice, keen to rekindle the romance, sent Morsby a pair of silver dice as a love token, via Adam Fowle, who lived at the Fleur de Lis inn near her house.

Arden, it seems, had discovered what was going on between his wife and Morsby, but turned a blind eye. One of the earliest accounts of the murder, taken from the *Wardmote Book of Faversham* (essentially the official town records) tells us that Morsby was subsequently not only kept in their house, but that Alice fed him 'with delicate meats' and bought him 'sumptuous apparel.' Holinshed tells us that this state of affairs went on for some time, but that Arden put up with the shenanigans going on under his nose as he did not wish to fall out with his wife or her friends. Perhaps, most importantly, he feared falling out of favour with the powerful Sir Edward North. At any rate Arden was, so Holinshed records, 'contented to wink at her filthy disorder.'

Eventually, however, the affair was not enough for Alice who wanted Arden out of the way so that she could marry Morsby. Holinshed says that she, 'at length, inflamed in love with Mosbie, and loathing her husband, wished and after practised the means how to hasten his end.'

Arden was far from popular in Faversham. The ease with which he had accumulated so much land in the town had attracted the ire of other leading local figures. According to Holinshed, he had even cheated a widow out of the land where his dead body would eventually be found. Arden's avarice finally got the better of him when he was said to have arranged for the upcoming St Valentine's Fair to be held entirely on his own land, rather than letting the rest of the town in on the financial rewards. It was the last straw for other local dignitaries who, in December 1550, booted him out of his local offices, disenfranchising him completely.

Perhaps Arden's unpopularity was one reason why his wife found it relatively easy to draw others into her dastardly plans for his downfall. In fact, she would later try and convince Morsby to join the murder plot on the basis that no-one would care about Arden's death or make 'anie great inquirie for them that should dispatch him.'

Alice's initial attempt to do away with her husband involved poison, which she got with the help of a painter, William Blackbourne. This ploy had failed, according to Holinshed, as Arden simply threw up the potion and recovered. Now Alice managed to inveigle others into her web of intrigue. First she targeted a tailor, John Green, who had been involved in a local property dispute with her husband. Alice promised Green ten pounds if he could come up with a way of getting rid of her husband.

Soon, Green made a journey up from Faversham to Gravesend and took a local goldsmith by the name of George Bradshaw with him for company. On the way, near Rochester, they happened to bump into a well-known villain known as Black Will, from Calais, with whom Bradshaw had once served in the army on the continent. Green invited the 'terrible cruell ruffian' who was armed with a sword to sup with them and later hired him to kill Arden. He immediately wrote to Alice saying: 'We have got a man for our purpose.' Meanwhile Green also managed to recruit one of Arden's own disgruntled servants, Michael Saunderson, into the conspiracy. While Arden was up in London on business, Green convinced Saunderson to leave the doors of the property where he was staying unbolted so Black Will could sneak in and murder him there. But Saunderson got cold feet, fearing he too would be killed and so the plan failed. On two more occasions, Black Will and a side-kick called Losebagg (George Shakebag in Holinshed) lay in wait for Arden in the countryside as their target went about his business, but they were again thwarted in their quest, by one obstacle or another.

Morsby, who was not yet persuaded that murder was the right course of action, now offered to pick a fight with Arden at the St Valentine's Fair, presumably with the hope that Arden would die in the affray or challenge him to a duel. But he and Alice decided that this wouldn't work since

Arden had always remained phlegmatic when Morsby had tried to goad him in the past.

Alice now arranged a secret conference of the conspirators at the house of Morsby's sister, Cecily Pounder, which was near her own home. In attendance were Morsby, Pounder, John Green, Black Will and Losebagg, Michael Saunderson and a maid (perhaps the Elizabeth Stafford mentioned in the Wardmote Book). They discussed how best to do away with Arden once and for all. At first, Morsby refused to be a part of the scheme and 'in a furie floong awaie' making his way to the Fleur de Lis inn where he often lodged. Alice sent a messenger after Morsby urging him to return, which he eventually did. Holinshed says that, 'at his comming backe she fell downe upon his knees to him and besought him to go through with the matter as if he loved her he would be content to do.' Finally she convinced him to take part.

That evening, at about seven o'clock, while Arden was out on business, Alice sent away most of the servants at their home – apart from those who were in on the plot. When the coast was clear, Black Will was ushered into the house and concealed in a 'closet' at the end of the parlour. When Arden returned home, Morsby met him on the doorstep and Arden asked him if dinner was ready. Morsby told him that it wasn't and the two agreed to play a few games of backgammon in the parlour. The Tudor form of the game was then known as 'playing at tables' and was extremely popular.

Holinshed's account of the murder has Arden sitting down in the parlour at the gaming table, with his back to the closet where Black Will was hiding. Michael Saunderson now stood behind Arden with a candle watching the game, further throwing a shadow on to the adjoining room where Black Will lay waiting for a signal. The conspirators had agreed on a verbal cue to let the hired assassin know that it was his moment to attack.

After a little while Morsby said to Arden: 'Now may I take you sir if I will.'

'Take me?' Replied Arden studying the board curiously, 'Which way?'

Suddenly Black Will appeared. *The Wardmote Book* tells us that he, 'came with a napkin in his hand, and sodenlye came behind the said Ardern's back, threw the said napkin over his hedd and face, and strangled him.' Now Morsby got in on the act and, stepping towards Arden struck him 'with a taylor's great pressing iron upon the scull to the braine.'

Holinshed tells us that the iron weighed fourteen pounds and that after he had been struck with it Arden 'fell downe, and gave a great grone.' According to *The Wardmote Book,* Morsby then 'immediately drew out his dagger, which was great and broad, and therewith cut the said Ardern's throat.'

In Holinshed's version, Arden was carried out to the counting house but was not yet dead and gave another groan. It was Black Will, not Morsby, who set about him with a blade, gashing Arden in the face. He 'killed him out of hand.' Black Will then looted Arden's body taking, 'the monie out of his purse and the rings from his fingers' before demanding his fee too. Alice paid the assassin his ten pounds and Black Will left. Then she returned to her husband's body and herself gave it seven or eight 'pricks' with a knife for good measure. The Wardmote Book has a slightly different version in which Black Will got his pay-off at Cecily Pounder's house.

The murderous party now set about covering their tracks, cleaning the house of blood. But they do not seem to have given much consideration over what they were going to do with Arden's body. *The Wardmote Book* tells us that they bore the corpse into a meadow adjoining the back of Arden's garden. Here it appears to have been unceremoniously dumped – probably with the hope that his murder would be put down to some stranger attending the fair. Holinshed's account reveals that Saunderson, Pounder, a maid and Arden's daughter were those that carried the body into the field and that as they did so it began to snow. They then discovered they had forgotten the garden gate key and had to go back for it. Finally they laid Arden 'down on his back straight in his night-gown, with his slippers on' and left him in the long grass.

Once they had returned to the house and the other servants were summoned back to it, Alice had the gumption to entertain some visiting businessmen, pretending that Arden was simply late home. As time went on she made a show of getting worried about his whereabouts and, later that evening, sent entreaties around the town asking where her husband might be.

Later that night a search was launched, led by the new mayor himself. Unsurprisingly it wasn't long before Arden's body was found by a grocer called Prune, who apparently simply stumbled across the corpse in the gloom. Arden was quickly judged to have been 'thoroughly dead'. Thanks to the snow, which the hapless murderers hadn't counted on, the search party 'espied certeine footsteps...betwixt the place where he laie and the garden doore.'

The mayor and his men immediately went to Arden's house and quizzed both Alice and her servants. Whether or not his peers liked Arden, Alice had been sorely mistaken in thinking that they would not bother to probe his death. Given the cack-handedness of the crime, the mayor and the other men now had no choice but to find out what had happened. At first, Alice and her accomplices denied any knowledge of the murder. But the investigators not only discovered tell-tale blood and hair at the scene but the knife which had been used to kill Arden, as well as a bloodied cloth in the 'tub'. Being presented with these items Alice knew that the game was up and confessed. She and the other members of the household who had helped her were promptly put in prison. Alice does not seem to have hesitated in implicating her own lover. That very night, Morsby was picked up at the Fleur de Lis inn where he was found in bed. In the room there was more incriminating evidence in the form of his hose and purse which was 'stained with some of Master Arden's bloud.' He too confessed and was put behind bars awaiting a specially convened court.

The trial of Alice and her co-conspirators took place just weeks later at the very abbey hall that Arden had recently bought. Here they were 'adjudged to dye'.

Alice was burned at the stake in nearby Canterbury on 14 March, 1551. The fate of the others was equally uncompromising. Elizabeth Stafford was burned at the stake too, in Faversham. Morsby was hanged at Smithfield in London along with his sister, while Michael Saunderson's sentence was to be 'drawn and hanged in chains within the liberties of Faversham'. George Bradshaw, despite pleading no knowledge of the conspiracy (probably with some justification) was nevertheless hanged in chains at Canterbury. Meanwhile something of a national manhunt was launched to find the other conspirators.

Finally, in July 1551, John Green was tracked down in Cornwall and returned to Faversham where he was hanged. Both Black Will and the mysterious Losebagg remained at large having presumably fled back to the continent. Holinshed reports that Black Will was arrested in 1553 and later 'burned on a scaffold' at Flushing in the Netherlands (modern day Vlissingen). William Blackbourne, the painter, seems to have remained at large. Adam Fowle, the innkeeper at the Fleur de Lis, was at first implicated and taken in shackles to London, but later released. No more

Arden's house in Faversham as is is today.

mention is made of Alice's daughter and her possible involvement.

The intense drama of the murder was caught in a woodcut included in the frontispiece to *Arden of Faversham*, which emerged in 1592. It shows the very act itself, with Black Will strangling Arden while Alice hovers in the background with a dagger. The play itself fleshed out the characters of Alice and Arden, but the bones of the story were drawn from the facts. Debate still rages as to whether Shakespeare really did write it – Thomas Kyd and Christopher Marlowe have also been put forward as candidates. It was certainly written by an adept author, who had probably read Holinshed's account of the murder. The case was never forgotten in Faversham and local legend has it that, for two years after the terrible event, the grass would not grow on the spot where Arden's dead body was found.

Plaque recording the murder at Arden's House.

Chapter 10

Ambushed by the Red Bandits 1555

In the village of Mallwyd, located in a lonely part of Gwynedd, Wales, is an old hostelry called the Brigands' Inn. Its name recalls a local band of rogues who terrorised the local countryside in the sixteenth century. The area had a reputation as a lawless region, home to a notorious group called the Gwylliaid Cochion Mawddwy or the Red Bandits of Mawddwy, who supposedly got their name thanks to the fact that many of them had red hair. This was high, rugged country on the borders of the old Principality of Wales and the Welsh Marches, territory in which the ruling classes had long struggled to establish control.

But Wales was changing. With the imposition of a new regime, there were determined men bent on bringing to an end the terror which pervaded the region. Since 1282, Wales had effectively been annexed by England and those running the Principality of Wales were appointed by the English crown. Under the Tudors, however, the process of unification would go even further. The dynasty itself did, of course, have its roots there. The first Tudor king, Henry VII, was the descendant of a powerful family from Anglesey. Concerned that Wales might pose a threat right on his doorstep, Henry VIII sought to accelerate the process of Anglicisation.

Between 1535 and 1542, the Laws in Wales Acts were passed, extending the legal system of England into the Principality of Wales and the Marcher Lordships (small buffer states between England and Wales). These reforms meant that Welsh MPs would now sit in the English parliament and a re-defined Wales would be divided up into English style counties. A similar court system was introduced, while sheriffs and justices of the peace were appointed to administer the law. It was further decreed that English would be the only language allowed in the law courts and speaking it was a pre-requisite to holding any official position.

Lewis Owen was one of the men at the forefront of the new Wales.

He had come from a well-established family that could claim to be related to the nation's old princes. But he saw that the English reforms would bring members of the Welsh gentry such as himself more rights, power and wealth. The new regime would also allow the ruling elite to take a tighter grip on the country. Owen and his peer group accepted the subjugation of Welsh tradition and culture in return for a more orderly, modern state. In the longer term, the changes caused social divisions to widen, not least because the rulings on language had ignored the fact that most of the nation's ordinary folk spoke only Welsh.

It is believed that Owen was born around 1500, the eldest son of Owen ap Hywel ap Llywelyn and came from near Dolgellau, where the family had a house called Cwrt Plas-yn-dre. He married Margaret Puleston in about 1540 and must have had some legal training as, by the 1540s, he was appointed to some important posts in the wake of Henry's administrative shake-up. In 1543, Owen became a justice of the peace for Merionethshire and, in 1545, a sheriff of the county. He would also become a vice-chamberlain of North Wales and a baron of the exchequer at Caernarvon, a role involving the administration of local finances. Baron Owen was one of the first people to be made a Welsh MP and he built up large estates in the area around Dollgelau, acquiring other benefits such as the fishing rights of the coastal town of Barmouth. His estate was worth £300 a year.

In 1554, Owen, as sheriff, teamed up with another leading local figure and MP, Sir John Wynn ap Meredydd to try and impose order on Merionethshire. No doubt the Red Bandits played havoc with the profits from their estates and there was much self-interest in their campaign. But they had obtained an official commission and 'in pursuance of these orders, they raised a body of stout men.'

It would be a tough task to rid the region of the Red Bandits, who were a well organised and ruthless bunch of hardened criminals. It was said that their original 'captains' had once been men of property who could command 'eighty hearths' but that these men had fallen on hard times. It is possible that they had been formed following the turmoil of the Wars of the Roses in the previous century or from outlaws who had fled other parts of the realm.

The bandits were a huge headache, specialising in violent robbery, as well as stealing sheep and cattle. Much of our information on them comes from the writer Thomas Pennant, who tells us that they would 'rob and murder in large bands, setting defiance at the civil power and driving whole herds of cattle from one county to another in mid-day with the utmost impunity.' Pennant goes on to tell us that the Red Bandits, 'were so feared, that travellers did not dare to go the common road to Shrewsbury, but passed over the summits of the mountains, to avoid their haunts.'

Eventually, by Christmas 1554, Owen and Wynn's campaign had some success. They captured around 100 of the bandits who were thrown in jail. Before long as many as eighty of their number were sentenced to death. The executions were carried out on moorland near Mallwyd that has since been called Rhos Goch or the red moor. Legend has it that an incensed mother of two of the bandits, named Lowri, pleaded for her sons to be spared but that Owen refused. Furious, she bared her bosom at him saying: 'These breasts have nurtured other sons who will wash their hands in your heart's blood.' If this anecdote is true, it is unlikely that Owen, himself the father of seven sons and four daughters paid much attention to the woman's threat. Perhaps he should have done, for the Red Bandits were now out for revenge.

In October 1555, Owen set out for Montgomeryshire to attend the assizes in Welshpool and discuss a marriage between his heir, John, and Ursula the daughter of another local dignitary, Richard Mytton. It was on his way home, on the evening of 11 October, that several score of the bandits took up position near dense woodland above the road about three miles east of Malwydd, since known as Llydiart y Barwn. They had cut down trees to block the road. When Owen and his party halted at the obstacle, a shower of arrows suddenly rained down upon them from the hidden attackers. One caught Owen in the face, but he managed to pull it out and prepared to fight. The bandits then descended on the men with daggers and swords, bills and javelins. The baron's entourage fled and he was left with just his son-in-law John Lloyd for company. Though he fought bravely, Owen was eventually cut down. One of the bandits, by the name of John ap Gruffudd ap Huw is reckoned to have delivered the fatal blow, but when Owen's body was discovered it was found to have around thirty separate wounds.

The killing only made the authorities more determined to seek the extermination of the gang and one by one they were hunted down with many sent to the gallows. Pennant tells us that the 'most rigorous justice ensued and the whole nest of banditti was extirpated, many by the hand of justice; and the rest fled, never to return.' In 1558, Lowri herself was brought to trial but pleaded pregnancy to avoid the noose. This claim was found to be true and she managed to avoid the death penalty.

Chapter 11

Hanged by a Rope Made of Silk 1557

On the morning of Saturday 6 March, 1557, in the market place of Salisbury in Wiltshire, a peer of the realm met his end in a unique fashion. Lord Stourton was granted the distinction that his noose be made of silk rather than suffer the usual form of hanging with a halter made from hemp. It has been suggested that this might have made the process kinder as 'the smaller the rope, the more sudden and complete is the strangulation, especially as the smoother material causes the noose to close more effectually upon the windpipe.' If he enjoyed a more elegant end than some of those who found themselves on the gallows, it was in stark contrast to the crimes for which Stourton was executed, ones which exhibited the casual brutality of a man who considered murder as simply a convenient method of getting his own way.

Charles Stourton was a man who bore grudges. His first was towards his own father, William, the 7th Baron Stourton, who had a grand house at Stourton (now known as Stourhead) in Wiltshire and large estates across four counties. In 1539, William had written to Thomas Cromwell describing his heir as a 'false hypocrite' worthy of imprisonment. One of the issues of contention between them was undoubtedly that for years William had shunned his wife and Charles' mother, Elizabeth, for the charms of another woman, Agnes ap Rhys, the daughter of an important Welsh landowner. William was primarily a military man, who spent much of his time abroad in the service of Henry VIII, comforted by Agnes.

During his time away in France in the 1540s, Stourton senior had entrusted the stewardship of his West Country estates to William Hartgill, another member of the local landed gentry. Hartgill, who resided in the neighbouring parish of Kilmington in Somerset, may have been a couple of notches down the social scale but he was relatively successful. He had served as an MP and was described as a 'mighty, stout' person. Elsewhere, however, he's alleged to have been a 'surly dogged, crosse fellowe' who was rapacious when it came to acquiring wealth and new land for his family.

At some point towards the end of the decade relations between the 7th Baron and Hartgill became tense in disputes over property. Stourton wrote a letter to Hartgill saying that he had been given reports that 'yowe seeke youre owne gayne more than my comodytie and honour.' Then, in September 1548, Stourton died while still abroad, leaving a large bequest of his belongings to Agnes, incensing his son Charles, who now became the 8th Baron.

The fate of his mother now became the cause of Charles' next big grudge. He was worried that if Elizabeth married again, some of his estates might be lost. She had been lodging at Hartgill's house as his guest during her husband's years abroad. Stourton asked for Hartgill's help in persuading Elizabeth to make an agreement that she would not marry again and would give up the right to any of his lands in return for an annuity. Hartgill demanded better terms for Elizabeth and no agreement was made. Stourton was furious, though it probably hadn't helped that he'd already sacked Hartgill from the post of steward. Stourton 'fell utterly owt' with the said William Hartgill and was soon seeking revenge.

On a Sunday morning, in May 1549, he and 'a great many men with bowes and gunnes' came to Kilmington Church where William Hartgill and family were at prayer. Being told that Stourton's men were outside, William's son John realised that his family would need weapons with which to defend themselves. Being 'a tall lusty gentleman' he rushed out of the church with his sword drawn, making for his father's house, which was nearby. Some of Stourton's men suddenly started firing off arrows in John's direction, but they missed their target. Meanwhile William Hartgill, now a relatively elderly man, was forced to retreat up the church tower for his own safety along with his wife and some of their servants.

At the house John 'toke his longe bowe and arrows … and charged a gonne.' Getting one of the female servants to carry some of the weapons for him, he now went outside again and managed to draw off Stourton's men, shooting one of them in the shoulder. Stourton's party retreated and John took his chance to race into the church. He asked his father what they should do next. William said that he and the family would remain in the church tower for safety while he should make with all haste to London and tell the Privy Council 'how I am used'. Hartgill clearly had little faith in local lawkeepers, with many of the justices of the peace effectively in Stourton's pocket. John arranged for food and drink to be brought up to the church tower and rode off to London.

He arrived in the capital on the Monday evening and swiftly got an audience with the Privy Council, informing them what had happened. They ordered Sir Thomas Speake, the Sheriff of Somerset, to go and free the Hartgills and bring Stourton to London to answer for his actions. Speake arrived at Kilmington on the Wednesday, where he found Stourton and his men still besieging the tower, although they had let William Hartgill's wife Joan go home. In the meantime, Stourton's men had also stolen and shot Hartgill's prize gelding, while the Baron put it about that the Hartgills had been poaching on his land.

Stourton was only detained briefly at the Fleet prison in London and was soon back in Wiltshire harrying the Hartgills. A contemporary account tells us that he 'contynued his mallice' throughout Edward's reign and 'with violence and force toke from the sayd William Hartgyll all the corn and catall that he could any way come bye.' In July 1553, Queen Mary acceded to the throne and the Catholic-leaning Stourton was made Lord Lieutenant of Wiltshire, Somerset and Dorset.

Meanwhile, others suffered at the hands of Stourton, including Thomas Chaffyn, a local gentleman. His servants were assaulted, his crops stolen and his barn burned down. In fact, one observer claimed that Stourton's 'ryottes, robberyes and murdres … were to long to wright.' The Hartgills, for their part, appealed to the queen for redress. Stourton was eventually ordered by the Council to give back some of the goods he had taken from them. If the Hartgills would come to his house, Stourton said, he would arrange it. The Baron had no intention of doing any such thing. On the way to Lord Stourton's property, the Hartgills and another man were ambushed in a narrow lane by 'six ruffians'. John Hartgill was left badly injured.

The matter now came to the Star Chamber, a body composed of senior privy councillors. The authorities were clearly beginning to find Stourton's behaviour rather tiresome. In late 1556, he was put in the Fleet again and ordered to pay damages of more than £368 – a huge sum – to the Hartgills. He was released from prison on a surety of £2,000 and asked to reappear in January 1557 to show the money had been paid out.

Four days after arriving home Stourton sent a message to the Hartgills saying he was ready to pay up and hoped for the 'quyeting of all matters between them.' Given past form, the Hartgills were understandably sceptical that Stourton was genuine about ending their feud. But when he suggested that they meet on 'home turf' at Kilmington church to make payment they agreed.

The meeting was set for Monday 11 January. Stourton arrived at Kilmington with a huge number of servants and supporters, including friendly members of the local gentry. The sight of such a large party, around forty strong, filled the Hartgills with dread and they headed for the church. Meanwhile, Stourton took up position in the adjoining church-house, sending a message to the Hartgills that he felt the church was no place to discuss 'worldelye matters'. A wary William Hartgill came out and stood within twenty paces of Stourton saying, 'I see many ennemyes of myne about your Lordship and therefore I ame very moch afrayed to come anny nere.' Eventually, it was agreed that a table should be set up in the open. The Hartgills were still cautious but Stourton appeared to place a purse of gold on the table, promising to pay every penny that the court had ordered. The Hartgills now approached Stourton but when they were near enough to grab he cried out, 'I arrest you both for felony'. Then twelve of his men stepped forward, overpowering William and John Hartgill and violently bundling them into the church house, where Stourton quickly relieved them of their purses.

Stourton ordered his men to bind the arms of the Hartgills behind their backs. When John Hartgill protested about how he and his father were being treated Stourton gave him a 'great blowe' to shut him up. Going outside with his sword drawn, Stourton also struck out at John Hartgill's wife with his spurs, ripping her hose. He then struck her 'betwen the neck and the hedd' with his blade. She fell to the floor and was taken away barely clinging to life.

Stourton's two prisoners were then taken to the parsonage at Kilmington where they were kept for the rest of the day 'withowte meate or drincke'. Stourton considered murdering his captives there and then but was persuaded otherwise by one of his men. At about one or two o'clock in the morning, the Hartgills were then moved to a farmhouse on Stourton's estate, a couple of miles from his mansion. For the next twelve hours they were given nothing to eat or drink or any bed to lie on.

The following afternoon, Stourton sent for two justices of the peace to come and examine the Hartgills. What exactly they were alleged to have done, or what Stourton's purpose was in having them arrested, has not been recorded. The justices advised Stourton that the prisoners should be unbound as they were not likely to be able to escape. But they were afraid of upsetting such a powerful local figure and failed to order that the pair should be immediately taken to gaol as was proper. They left, apparently with Stourton's assurance that the Hartgills would be delivered to the prison the next day.

It's hard to know what was going on in Stourton's mind at this point but it appears that he now entirely resolved to kill the Hartgills. It's possible that he had got the impression that the justices were not convinced that the Hartgills had a case to answer and even that they might turn the tables and accuse him instead. Perhaps he saw an opportunity in what the justices had said about their ties so he could now kill the Hartgills and more convincingly explain their sudden disappearance by claiming that they had escaped. In fact, as soon as the justices had left, Stourton got his men to tie the Hartgills up again.

By ten o'clock on the Tuesday evening, he had sent four handpicked servants, William Farre, Roger Gough, John Welshman and Macute Jacob to fetch the Hartgills from the farmhouse where Henry Symes was watching them. With their arms still tied behind their backs the Hartgills were brought up to the main manor house. Here, just outside the walls, they were 'knocked in the heads with two clubbes wherewith, kneling on their hands fast bounde behind them, being at one stroke felled, they received afterward sondry strokes' until the murderers thought them dead. Records show that Farre had struck William first and Henry Symes had then beaten John. Stourton was overseeing all this from a nearby doorway. The servants then wrapped up the Hartgills in gowns and started to carry them inside. Suddenly one of the servants tripped up on a hole and tumbled to the ground with William Hartgill, who let out a groan. In fact, neither of the Hartgills were quite dead and Symes told Stourton that they ought to be put out of their pains. Stourton, worried that some of the other occupants of the house might be woken up by the noise, agreed. William Farre then 'tooke owte his knyfe and cut bothe their throotes.' Stourton held a candle to help him see what he was doing. Realising the gravity of what he had done, one of the murderers now showed regret for the act saying, 'Ah my Lorde! This is a pytiouse sight.' Stourton reprimanded him saying that being rid of two such knaves should be considered no more than the killing of two sheep.

The bodies of the Hartgills were then thrown down into a cellar under the house which Symes and Gough had to be lowered into. Hurriedly they dug out a pit in which to bury the corpses. Stourton urged them on saying, 'Make speede, for that the night went away.' The Hartgills ended up entombed '15ft deep'. A 'double pavement' was placed on top of them along with shavings and sawdust to conceal signs of the burial.

All this was unknown to the family of the Hartgills who had meanwhile sent a swift appeal to the Privy Council for the immediate release of their kinsmen. The Council acted promptly, ordering Stourton to deliver his captives to the Sherriff of Somerset and to come to London to explain himself.

Within days, Stourton was locked up at the Fleet prison. Brought before the Privy Council, his fine for his former transgressions was increased to which Stourton spat back, 'I am sorie to see that retorick doth rule where law should take place.' The Lord Chancellor told him that he had slandered the court and promised to inform the queen of his behaviour.

Stourton was then quizzed as to the whereabouts of the Hartgills who were nowhere to be found. The lying Baron claimed to have delivered them to a constable and suggested that they must have escaped from him. The court thought it a pathetic story and, suspecting foul play, committed Stourton to the Tower where he arrived on 28 January. Soon the servants thought to have aided him were languishing there too. Acting on information from one of them, Sir Anthony Hungerford, the Sherriff of Wiltshire, ordered a search of Stourton's property. He must have been told where to find the bodies, because the corpses of the Hartgills were soon unearthed.

On the 17 February, Stourton was brought to Westminster to hear the evidence gathered against him and was found unable to deny it. He was finally arraigned at Westminster Hall on 26 February, facing a charge of murder. Even though he had not himself done the deed, he was deemed to be equally responsible. Stourton refused to enter a plea at his trial in front of a jury made up of other peers. He probably took this course of action hoping that his family's lands would not be confiscated. It was then pointed out to him by the Lord Chief Justice that the penalty for not answering the charge was to be 'pressed to death' (see page 19). Chastened, Stourton now 'expressly acknowledged the said felony and murder and for the same placed himself in the mercy of the Queen.'

If Stourton was expecting his Papist leanings would see him granted a pardon from Mary, he was to be sorely disappointed. She appears to have lost patience with Stourton, who had been granted plenty of slack over the years for his misdemeanours. It was said that 'since she left her friends to the law, her enemies had no reason to complain of the execution of it upon them.' Stourton was even denied the aristocratic privilege of being beheaded. Instead he would be hanged.

On 2 March, Stourton was taken to Salisbury, back in Wiltshire, in the custody of Sir Robert Oxenbridge and guards. He made the journey on horseback 'with his arms pinioned, and his legs tied under the horse'. The Baron was hanged in the market place four days later where he made 'great lamentation at his death for his wilful and impious deeds'. Meanwhile, four of the servants that had helped Stourton physically carry out the murder were also taken back to Salisbury, put on trial and found guilty. At least one of them was hanged at the village of Mere, near to the scene of the murder. All were gibbeted in chains.

While the Hartgill family received a small measure of financial compensation for the deaths of William and John Hartgill, Stourton's four year old heir, John, did not fare too badly. Most of Stourton's property was bought back from the crown thanks to the efforts of his wife Anne, who appealed directly to Mary bemoaning the loss of her 'loving, trew and faithfull' husband. John Stourton swiftly became the 9th Baron Stourton.

Chapter 12

The Body at the Bottom of
the Stairs
1560

In 1810 a ruinous house called Cumnor Place, in Oxfordshire, was finally pulled down. Legend has it that one of the reasons that this once grand home had fallen into disrepair, and for its demolition, was that it was haunted by the restless soul of a former occupant, Amy Robsart. Since Amy's lifeless body was discovered at the bottom of the stairs in the house on Sunday 8 September, 1560, exactly what happened to her has been the subject of fevered speculation. And the mystery surrounding her sudden death remains as potent more than 400 years on as it was in the Elizabethan era with many still believing that the 28-year-old was callously murdered.

Cumnor Place dated back to the fourteenth century and had been in the possession of Abingdon Abbey before the dissolution. By the time Amy moved in, during December 1559, it was being leased to Sir Anthony Forster. He was an associate of Robert Dudley the dashing gentleman Amy had married with great pomp and ceremony at the royal palace at Sheen back in 1550, when they were both just eighteen. Amy, described as 'beautiful' by one Elizabethan source, had been born in 1532 and was from a well-heeled background – the only child of Sir John Robsart, Sheriff of Norfolk and Suffolk. Dudley was from an extremely powerful family, being the son of the Duke of Northumberland who had risen to power under Henry VIII and his son Edward.

It seems that initially the couple were very much in love, but shortly after their union Dudley ended up in the Tower of London, through his involvement in the unsuccessful attempt to have Lady Jane Grey declared queen. Narrowly avoiding execution, he spent months in prison. Dudley eventually worked himself back into favour with the new queen, Mary,

The death of Amy Robsart. Illustration by WF Yeames for *The Graphic*, 29 September, 1877 (Copyright Look and Learn)

but had financial difficulties and, in the following years, spent a good deal of time abroad fighting the French. He and Amy spent a lot of time living apart and the couple had no children together.

Once Elizabeth had acceded to the throne in 1558, Dudley's fortunes soared. They had been childhood friends and Dudley was immediately made Master of the Horse, his equine responsibilities including everything from organising military operations to tournaments and even helping the monarch off her steed when hunting. He quickly became one of Elizabeth's favourite courtiers and continued to spend a lot of time away from home, especially as the sovereign discouraged wives from attending court. Dudley did, however, keep Amy well supplied with gifts and she received income from his estates. She kept her own household, complete with around ten servants, periodically moving between different homes owned by friends and family across the South of England.

Early into Elizabeth's reign there were rumours that the unmarried Elizabeth had fallen in love with Dudley. In April 1559, the Spanish ambassador, Count de Feria, wrote: 'During the last few days, Lord Robert has come so much into favour that he does whatever he likes with affairs. It is even said that Her Majesty visits him in his chamber day and night.' His successor, Alvaro de la Quadra, said there was talk of Dudley divorcing Amy in order to marry the queen. There were even whispers that the pair had produced illegitimate offspring. There is no doubt that Amy would have been aware of the rumours surrounding her husband. Dudley spent less and less time with her. In fact, the last time he saw his wife before she died was in the summer of 1559.

On the morning of her death Amy sent all her servants off to a fair in Abingdon while she remained at Cumnor, apparently disgruntled that a fellow resident, Mrs Odingsells, insisted on staying behind. Also remaining was an elderly woman called Mrs Owen, who dined with Amy a little later. That afternoon, Amy's body was discovered by one of the household's servants who had returned from the fair. The two other women seem to have retired to their chambers and been unaware of anything untoward happening.

One of Dudley's retainers, a man called Bowes, who was present, immediately set off for Windsor Castle where Dudley was attending on the queen to inform him of the tragedy. The day after the murder, Dudley wrote an apparently anguished letter to his steward, Thomas Blount, who, coincidentally, had already left for the vicinity of Cumnor on business the

Portrait of Robert Dudley, by Jacobus Houbraken, 1738. Dudley was suspected of murdering his wife (Courtesy Wellcome Library, London)

day before. In the letter he says, 'There came to me Bowes, by whom I do understand that my wife is dead and as he sayeth by a fall from a pair of stairs. Little other understanding can I have of him. The greatness and the suddenness of the misfortune doth so perplex me.' He asked Blount to 'use all the devices and means you can possible for the learning of the troth' and asked him to make sure that the coroner chose the 'discreetist and most substantial men' for the jury to get to the 'bottom of the matter'. By the time Blount arrived on 10 September, the coroner had already sworn in the jury who had begun their investigations, viewing Amy's body at Cumnor. Soon, Blount was reporting to Dudley that, as far as he could tell, they could 'find no presumptions of evil'. His own enquires had led him to believe that 'misfortune hath done it and nothing else.'

The official coroner's report found that on leaving her bedroom Amy had descended by a set of 'steyres' and accidentally fell to the very bottom where she sustained two 'dyntes' on the head. One of these injuries was about an inch deep, the other two inches in depth. The impact of the fall had also broken Amy's neck the report found, the effect of which, according to the inquest jurors, was to have caused instantaneous death. There were no other marks on Amy's body. The conclusion was that Amy had died through 'misfortune'.

So was Amy's death simply an accident? While her injuries do seem to have been compatible with a fall, the lack of other bruising and the severity of the two deep gashes on her head seem suspicious. Of course, her wounds might have been exactly the same whether she had fallen or been pushed. Reports suggest that the stone flight of stairs which she was thought to have tumbled down may have had as few as eight steps. If Amy died from an accidental fall, had she simply tripped on her dress, missed her footing or was there another cause?

There is some evidence that Amy was unwell and that this might have caused a sudden fall. In his letter of April 1559, de Feria had referred to 'a malady in one of her breasts' adding that court gossip had it that 'the Queen is only waiting for her to die to marry Lord Robert.' This has led to the suggestion that Amy might have been suffering from breast cancer which had spread to her bones. It's thought that this might have made them fragile, causing the vertebrae in her neck to suddenly snap while she was descending the stairs. Yet there is no firm evidence that Amy was gravely ill. While one ambassador says she has been 'ailing for some time' another report states that she was 'not ill at all, she was very well'.

Could Amy's mental health have been to blame? It has been suggested that her despair at the romance between Dudley and Elizabeth could have led her to suicide. Whether she was still in love with Dudley or not, the situation might certainly have put her under a lot of stress. She may have believed her life was in peril. Tellingly, when Blount had arrived at Cumnor he quizzed Amy's personal maid, Pirto, asking her if she thought Amy's death was 'chance or villainy' to which she replied, 'by very chance, and neither done by man or herself' but added that she had heard Amy 'pray to God to deliver her from desperation'. When Blount asked if her mistress might have had an 'evil toy' in her mind she backtracked. She was careful not to imply that Amy had committed suicide which was, after all, both a crime and a sin. Writing to Dudley, Blount spoke of 'divers tales that had made him think her 'a strange woman of mind.'

No-one could have blamed Amy for being depressed, but was she low enough to kill herself? Aside from the fact that throwing oneself down a stairwell is not a very reliable form of suicide, a key piece of evidence is that, just two weeks before her death, Amy wrote to her tailor ordering alterations to be made to a gown, not perhaps the actions of someone with self-murder in mind. Research by the Mayo Clinic in the United States has shown that the modern suicide rate for patients with depression is between just two and nine percent and there's no reason to think that it would have been much different in Tudor times. Indeed, given that most people were religious and suicide meant eternal damnation, rates might have been much lower. It's more likely that there is another explanation for Amy's untimely end.

Interestingly, the verdict of the inquest that Amy's death was misfortune was somewhat caveated by the phrase 'in so far as it is possible at present for them to agree' which leaves open the possibility of some other cause and suggests some heated debate among the jurors. For many who have analysed the case the essential problem with both the notion that Amy's death was an accident, perhaps caused by illness, or suicide is not only that the evidence is limited but that it just seems too convenient for a young woman like Amy to have suddenly perished in such a manner at a time when it would have been very useful to a number of people if she disappeared. It's also very possible that the wounds she suffered could have been inflicted by a weapon and that she had been placed at the bottom of the stairs to make it look like she had fallen. The possibility that Amy was murdered cannot be excluded.

Who might the perpetrator have been? Within days of Amy's death, rumours began to swirl that Amy had indeed been murdered. Thomas Lever, a senior member of the clergy in Coventry, wrote of, 'grievous and dangerous suspicion, and muttering.' Chief among the suspects was her own husband, Lord Robert. He was deemed to have the perfect motive, in that it would give him the freedom needed to marry the queen and there is little doubt that he was desperate to do so. In fact, even before her death, the idea that Robert planned to murder Amy was being discussed at the highest level. In November 1559, the Imperial ambassador Baron Bruener wrote: 'I have been told by many persons he is trying to do away with her by poison' while de Quadra spoke of Dudley sending poison to his wife and planning the 'wicked deed'. Indeed just days before Amy died, Elizabeth's chief advisor, William Cecil, told him that he understood Dudley was thinking of 'destroying' his wife. On the continent it was being taken as fact that Dudley was responsible, with Sir Nicholas Throckmorton, the English ambassador to France, lamenting how people there were amazed that Dudley could kill his wife and that the queen would not only 'bear withal but marry with him.' He added that even Mary Queen of Scots had joked that Elizabeth was about to 'marry her horse-keeper, who had killed his wife to make room for her.'

Dudley himself knew that Amy's death would reflect badly upon him. In his letter to Blount on hearing the news, he urges him to quickly find out how 'this evil should light upon me' as he knows there will be much gossip adding, 'I have no way to purge myself of the malicious talk that I know the wicked world will use.' His immediate concern for his own position may appear unseemly but his reaction to the death does seem to be one of genuine shock and a desire to know the truth. When it looked probable that the inquest would judge Amy's death accidental, he even spoke of organising an additional panel, to include Amy's half-brothers, to search for more evidence.

Nevertheless, it has been claimed that he was actually trying to sway the jury 'so shall it well appear to the world my innocency.' At one point the jury's foreman, Richard Smith, took the unusual step of writing to Dudley to reassure him that the verdict would be 'misfortune'. This man had been a servant of the queen herself which opens up the possibility that not only Dudley, but Elizabeth herself, was somehow involved in a conspiracy. Adding weight to this idea is one of de Quadra's letters, which seems to suggest that the queen had told him that Robert's wife was 'dead or nearly so' before the actual fact. A few days later, Elizabeth announced Amy's death to the court indicating it was an accident – before the inquest had completed its enquiries. In his talks with de Quadra, Cecil had also seemed to imply that both Dudley and the queen were involved in a plot to kill Amy.

Queen Elizabeth I, from an oil painting by Henry Gillard Glindoni. (Courtesy Wellcome Library, London)

While Dudley and Elizabeth might have had the motive to kill Amy, they were both too experienced politically not to know that if suspicion fell upon either of them, the ensuing scandal might make marriage impossible. This is, of course, exactly what happened. Elizabeth realised the potential damage to her reputation and while Dudley continued to be given titles

97

and honours, including being made the Earl of Leicester in 1564, the queen continued to blow 'bothe hote and colde' romantically with the eventual result that Dudley got married again, to someone else. Despite what he is reported to have said prior to Amy's death it is clear from other statements that even William Cecil didn't think Dudley was actually responsible for it.

Yet suspicions that Dudley did do it dogged him for the rest of his life. These sparked back into life dramatically in 1567, when John Appleyard, Amy's half-brother, raised again the view that his sister might have been murdered, with the implication that Dudley was behind it. He retracted the allegations after a short spell in prison and reading the official coroner's report. Later, in 1584, Catholic enemies of Dudley published a highly libellous pamphlet which became known as *Leicester's Commonwealth*. This claimed that one of Dudley's retainers, Sir Richard Verney, had gone to Cumnor under Dudley's orders to kill Amy and that he, along with another man, had broken Amy's neck before placing the body at the bottom of the stairs. Her hood was said to have been undisturbed about her head – a detail not recorded by the inquest. While the sensational accusations were built on a similar account, written in the 1560s, their author's motivation has to be in question, not least because *Leicester's Commonwealth* wildly accused Dudley of a string of other murders too.

Was there an attempt by those who did not want Dudley to marry Elizabeth to destroy his hopes by killing Amy? Many English nobles were set against the match and hoped that Elizabeth would marry one of the suitors from Europe's royal families busily vying for her hand. Perhaps the man who had most to gain was Cecil himself, who had recently been out of favour with the queen and thought her union with Dudley would bring 'manifest ruin'. He would certainly have had the power and contacts to make sure the murder was carried out in secret. Killing Dudley himself might be too obvious, but organising Amy's death would mean suspicion naturally fell on Dudley, especially after the rumours that Cecil had been spreading in the previous months. If Cecil *was* responsible, it was a big risk both for himself and his queen and might have the opposite effect in that she might marry Dudley after all. Cecil's stock certainly rose after the murder and ultimately he achieved his end in that the marriage never happened. In 1566, Cecil wrote to the Privy Council telling them that Dudley could not marry Elizabeth because he was 'infamed by the death of his wife.'

Portrait of Sir William Cecil, first Lord of Burghley, from a painting by Marcus Gheeraerts the younger in the Bodleian Library, Oxford - artist unknown. (Courtesy Wellcome Library, London)

Cecil is not the only one who might have been inclined to order Amy's assassination. Foul play by foreign powers or even other English candidates for Elizabeth's hand cannot be discounted. It's also possible that there was another culprit, one with a motive that remains unknown to history. This would explain why almost everyone involved seems to have been slightly wrong-footed by her sudden demise. Amy had virtually no relationship with Dudley at the time of her killing. Could she have a secret lover? Was that why she needed the velvet gown so urgently and the real reason she sent the servants away? Did they quarrel? Could the mysterious Mrs Odingsells or Mrs Owen, who seem to have been the last people known to have seen her alive, been hiding something?

Whatever the truth, Amy was buried in the Church of St Mary the Virgin at Oxford in a lavish funeral paid for by Dudley. He was not present, though nothing should be read into this as, in the sixteenth century, it was customary for the chief mourner to be of the same sex.

For many years afterwards, the chilling apparition of a beautiful woman at the bottom of the stairs caused consternation at Cumnor and even efforts by a string of parsons were said not to have been enough to exorcise Amy's ghost.

Chapter 13

Stabbed Fifty-Six Times
1566

Mary Queen of Scots was not lucky in love. Her first marriage, which was arranged for her, was to the sickly Francis II of France. He died in 1560 aged sixteen, just two years after their wedding. When Mary did choose a husband of her own it would be the handsome Henry Stuart, better known as Lord Darnley, a man who could claim Tudor descent (his mother was Margaret Tudor, daughter of Henry VII). But he would turn out to be a weak and feckless spouse who would later become convinced that Mary was having an affair with her private secretary – a man described by one contemporary as 'hideously ugly'.

Returning to Scotland from France in 1561, 18-year-old Mary took up the throne of the nation where she had been born. Her Catholicism, set against the rise of the Protestant religion which had become dominant in her absence, put her on course for conflict with many Scottish nobles and she struggled to govern the nation amid a multitude of warring factions. Mary's own half-brother, the Earl of Moray, was a leading Protestant and one of the most influential figures in the country. With the succession of the English throne always in question, Mary also had to tread a delicate diplomatic path with her father's cousin Elizabeth.

By 1565, Mary is said to have become 'bewitched' by the charms of Lord Darnley, a sometime Catholic who was technically an English subject and cousin of Elizabeth, who also had Scottish heritage. Against the English monarch's wishes, despite the fact that she had sent him north in the first place, Mary and Darnley were married that July. Yet, from the outset, the union was unsatisfactory. As king consort, Darnley had little interest in matters of state other than in securing his own position. As Mary tried to put down rebellious elements among her nobles, which even included Moray, Darnley spent much of his time drinking, hunting and whoring. That October, Mary fell pregnant but the relationship was already breaking down.

The increasingly arrogant Darnley now demanded to be awarded the Crown Matrimonial, meaning he would rule jointly with Mary. She refused and the relationship continued to sour as rumours circulated at court that Mary was sleeping with her hunchbacked secretary and confidante, David Riccio. A host of Scottish nobles now saw their chance to rid themselves of a troublesome Catholic queen and, despite his general unpopularity, turned to the easily-led Darnley as a useful pawn in their bid for power.

Riccio, born in about 1533, was an intriguing character. He originally came from Piedmont in Italy and, as a talented singer, had found his way into employment as one of the queen's musicians. His cultured nature soon caught the eye of Mary, who evidently found his love of cards and music a delightful diversion from dealing with the machinations of Scottish politics. However, many of the Protestant Scottish nobles felt that, promoted to the post of queen's secretary, Riccio was garnering too much power. Mary's relationship with Riccio was almost certainly more cerebral than carnal but that did not stop the gossip. Darnley became jealous as suspicions flew around that Riccio was the real father of Mary's unborn child. He and the rebels now plotted to murder Riccio, perceiving this foreigner as the symbol of everything that was wrong with Mary's reign.

There was some discussion about how it was to be done, with one suggestion being that Riccio might be thrown overboard during a fishing expedition. Instead, Darnley demanded that the act be perpetrated in a very public manner indeed – in front of the queen herself and at her chief residence, the Palace of Holyroodhouse in Edinburgh.

Darnley and the rebel lords went as far as signing a pact vowing to deal with the 'stranger Italian called Davie'. The agreement was that following the murder, the queen would be forced to give Darnley the Crown Matrimonial and then help protect the interests of Protestants, while former rebels would be forgiven. The key conspirators were to be: the Earl of Morton; Lord Ruthven; George Douglas the postulate; Lord Lindsay; Lord Ochiltree; the Earl of Glencairn; the Earl of Rothes; Lord Boyd and the Earl of Argyll. Also joining the plotters from afar was Moray, who had fled to England the previous year.

Riccio himself was aware that his life was in danger, but when an astrologer warned him to 'beware of the bastard', he dismissed the threat

The murder of David Riccio, from *The Murder of Rizzio*, by John Opie, 1787. (Courtesy of the Guildhall Art Library)

because he thought it referred to the exiled Moray – illegitimate son of James V. Riccio decided not to flee Scotland and so the die was cast. Mary seems to have been totally unaware of the murderous scheme. What happened next unleashed a chain of events that would eventually see all the major players dead or in exile.

On the evening of Saturday 9 March, the six months pregnant Mary was at her private supper chamber at Holyrood. This room, measuring just 12ft by 10ft, was part of her apartments on the second floor in the turreted northwest corner of the palace. Attending the meal were a handful of close associates, including her half-sister the Countess of Argyll, her half-brother Robert Stewart and Sir Arthur Erskine, along with some servants. Riccio was there too, dressed in a fine fur-lined damask robe, satin doublet and velvet hose.

Suddenly, at about 7pm, Darnley, who had played tennis with Riccio that very afternoon, made a surprise appearance. His rooms were below

Mary's and he entered via a private staircase and through a curtain that separated Mary's bedroom from the dining area. He and the queen did not usually eat together. Evidently bemused, the queen asked him if he had already dined and he replied that he had, casually putting his arm around Mary, kissing her and sitting next to her at the table.

Darnley gave no sign that he had just let his co-conspirators into the palace. They had with them a 100 strong force with which to overwhelm any guards and secure all the entrances. Around twenty had been stationed on the stairway leading to Mary's rooms. Shortly after Darnley had arrived Lord Ruthven burst into the supper room too. He must have made a striking sight, dressed in a cloak, with full armour underneath and a helmet on his head but still looking pale from an illness which, until now, had seen him laid up in bed. He told Mary that he had come to render her a service, 'To rid you of the villain who is at the end of the table and who merits neither place nor honour. We will not be governed by a varlet.' Another account has it that he said: 'Let it please your majesty that yonder man David come forth of your privy-chamber where he hath been overlong.'

Mary demanded to know what offence Riccio had committed and Ruthven replied that, 'he had offended your honour which I dare not be so bold as to speak of.' The implication was obvious. The reason for Darnley's visit must now have become clear to Mary – that he was involved in a dastardly plan to seize Riccio. Remaining remarkably composed, she offered that if Riccio had done wrong then the matter could more properly be dealt with before Parliament.

Ruthven ignored her and ordered Darnley to take hold of Mary, drawing his dagger. Some of those present tried to lunge towards Ruthven but he held them back saying, 'Lay no hands on me for I will not be handled.' More conspirators, Andrew Ker of Fawdonside, Patrick Bellenden, George Douglas, Thomas Scott and Henry Yair rushed in to aid him, brandishing blades and pistols.

In the ensuing commotion the table and most of the candles were knocked over. In the eerie gloom a cowering Riccio rushed to hide behind the queen herself, clinging to her dress. Fawdonside then pointed a pistol at Mary's bulging belly to which she is reported to have bellowed, 'Fire if you have no care for the child I carry in my womb.'

The distraught Riccio, now pleading with the queen to help save his life, is said to have been stabbed over Mary's shoulder, so close that she could actually feel the 'coldness of the steel' on her throat. Eventually wrestled from Mary's skirts, Riccio was dragged out of the room where more dagger wounds were inflicted on his body by countless conspirators, the secretary dying either in Mary's own bedroom or on the staircase where others rushed forward eager to land a blow.

It's thought that the first deadly thrust came from George Douglas, the illegitimate brother of the Earl of Morton, thus fulfilling the astrologer's earlier prophecy to Riccio. Douglas is said to have grabbed Darnley's own dagger to plunge into the Italian's body, leaving it sticking out of the side for all to see, so ensuring that the king would be complicit in the crime. Darnley himself had stayed behind in the supper room still restraining Mary, who feared that she too might now be murdered.

Riccio's lifeless corpse was thrown down to the bottom of the stairs and taken to the porters' lodge, where the fine clothes were ruthlessly stripped from it. His corpse was then unceremoniously buried in the graveyard attached to Holyrood Abbey.

After the murder, Mary was confined to her rooms and demanded to know of Darnley why he had orchestrated the 'wicked deed'. Darnley retorted that he felt usurped by Riccio. Meanwhile, an angry and armed crowd of local citizens had assembled outside the palace wanting to know what had happened. Fearing that the conspiracy might now unravel, Lindsay threatened Mary that she would be 'cut into collops' if she spoke to them. Instead Darnley appeared to reassure the mob that all was well and they dispersed. When Mary was later told that Riccio was definitely dead she vowed, 'No more tears, I will think upon a revenge.'

Mary was confined to her rooms. But by the next morning she had come up with a plan in the name of self-preservation and to protect her unborn child's claim to the throne. When a frightened Darnley came to her the next morning, worried that he could not trust the conspirators after all, she got him to tell her everything he knew about the plot. Slowly she managed to persuade Darnley that his best course of action was to pin his hopes on her fortunes, rather than of those with whom he had just colluded.

In the meantime, everything had not gone quite to plan for the conspirators. In all the commotion of the previous evening, and despite the palace being surrounded, two of Mary's then allies, the Earl of Bothwell and the Earl of Huntly, expecting to go the same way as Riccio, had managed to escape Holyrood – via the lion pit! The quick-thinking Mary now planned a similarly daring escape for herself and Darnley. By that Monday, she had led the conspirators to believe that she would forgive them for Riccio's death and co-operate with their demands. Then, using her pregnancy to feign illness, she retired to her rooms but not before managing to secure the help of a few loyal supporters. That night, she and Darnley managed to escape out of the private staircase at the back of the building and through some servants' quarters. On the way out they passed the very spot where Riccio had just been buried. Darnley apparently paused long enough to regret his killing, before he and Mary rendezvoused with a small escape party who were waiting for them with horses. After a five hour journey, they arrived at Dunbar Castle where Mary began planning what course of action to take next, writing a letter to Elizabeth describing the slaying of her 'special servant'. Reunited with Bothwell, Mary was able to rally more supporters among the nobility and within the space of just a few days had victoriously re-entered Edinburgh at the head of a large army. Darnley was at her side. Having been out-manoeuvred, most of the conspirators fled Scotland with Darnley declaring, 'As they have brewen so let them drink'. With bravado he issued a public proclamation that he'd personally had nothing to do with the murder plot.

The fate of the conspirators was mixed. A few were pardoned and Mary made her peace with Moray but upwards of sixty of the conspirators were declared outlaws and their lands confiscated. Morton and Ker escaped to England as did Ruthven, who wrote his own account of the murder before dying of natural causes that June in Newcastle. Just two individuals would actually be executed for their part in the murder: Thomas Scott, a man who was supposed to have had the job of protecting Mary at Holyrood and Henry Yair, who, not content with his part in the bloody end of Riccio, had promptly gone off and stabbed to death Adam Black, a friar. Yair and Scott were hanged, drawn and quartered.

Had the conspirators meant to kill Mary too? They certainly hadn't taken too much care of her safety on the night, but the intention was probably that with the death of Riccio she could be brought to heel. Mary herself always believed that her life had been in peril on that day, later telling Darnley: 'I have forgiven but will never forget! What if Fawdonside's pistol had shot, what would become of him and me both?' In time, Darnley would certainly get his comeuppance.

For a while Mary wrestled back full control of her nation and, on 19 June 1566 her son was born. He would go on to become James VI of Scotland and James I of England, but never quite shook off the taunts that he was actually Riccio's son, not Darnley's.

Portrait of Mary Queen of Scots by Jacobus Houbraken including a scene from her execution in February, 1587. (Courtesy Wellcome Library, London)

Chapter 14

A Royal Corpse Under a Pear Tree 1567

Lord Darnley, the great-grandson of Henry VII, was once described by his wife, Mary Queen of Scots as the 'lustiest and best proportioned long man' she had ever seen. When it came to the calibre of his political acumen however he was sorely deficient. Within months of their marriage he had begun plotting against Mary and been party to the murder of her private secretary, David Riccio, in March, 1566. Mary had shrewdly taken Darnley back afterwards to bolster her own position but she would never trust him again and within months his own life would be in danger.

After the death of Riccio, some of the conspirators who had fled Scotland sent Mary a copy of the bond which Darnley had signed, proving his part in the planning of the murder. This act of revenge, in retaliation for Darnley switching loyalties in the aftermath of the incident, could have left Mary in no doubt about his complicity. However, for reasons of political expediency she appeared to make a show of reconciliation with her husband, partly to ensure that her child, the future James VI, who was born that June, would be seen as a legitimate heir. Despite his weakened position Darnley demanded again that he rule as an equal, a position which Mary continued to deny him. Meanwhile she became closer to the pugnacious James Hepburn, the Earl of Bothwell, who became her chief military adviser and just possibly her lover too. Mary almost certainly couldn't bring herself to sleep with Darnley. Still aged only twenty, he sulked and was soon back to his bad old habits, drinking and carousing, even refusing to turn up to James' lavish baptism in December 1566 at Stirling Castle. During the course of the year, Mary had made peace with some of the rebels involved in the Riccio plot, including her own half-brother Moray and the Earls of Argyll and Glencairn but the deeply unpopular Darnley was increasingly seen as a problem by many of the lords, even those who were at loggerheads with each other.

A ROYAL CORPSE UNDER A PEAR TREE

Towards the end of 1566, a group of leading figures approached the queen at Craigmillar Castle, just outside Edinburgh, suggesting that a divorce from Darnley might be arranged, if she would pardon the remaining Ricco conspirators, including the Earl of Morton. Speed was of the essence they felt, or Darnley himself might take some dangerous course of action. The queen seemed open to their suggestions but insisted that any annulment or divorce should not threaten the legitimacy of her son. In one version of this meeting, William Maitland of Lethington reassured the queen not to worry and that they would 'find the means' to get rid of Darnley while Moray would 'look through his fingers' – the implication being that he would not stand in the way. Mary replied sharply that she hoped they would do 'nothing through which any spot may be laid upon mine honour'. Maitland suggested that she should allow them to 'guide the matter among us and your Grace shall see nothing but good and approved by Parliament.'

Like most aspects of Darnley's murder, the exact truth of what was discussed remains disputed but it seems that no explicit agreement was made with Mary. Yet, on Christmas Eve, Morton was duly pardoned along with another seventy accomplices from the Riccio murder. It is claimed that he, along with other nobles, such as Maitland, Bothwell, Argyll as well as the Earl of Huntly and the lawyer James Balfour, then drew up a bond by which they vowed that Darnley should be 'put off by one way or another'.

Realising he was now in some danger, Darnley went to stay with his relations in Glasgow but fell ill, probably with syphilis. Then, in January, Mary intervened. She went to Glasgow and brought Darnley back to Edinburgh – ostensibly so that he could convalesce from his illness near her. By 1 February he was housed, not at Craigmillar as Mary had initially wanted, but at a modest two storey building owned by Balfour's brother, known as the Old Provost's house in the church quadrangle at Kirk o' Field. The location, which Darnley preferred, was just inside the city wall. It was less than a mile from Holyrood, where Mary was in residence, though in the following days she often stayed the night at the house, overseeing Darnley's care.

On 9 February, Mary attended a wedding during the day then visited Darnley with some members of her court. Later that evening, she abruptly returned to Holyrood for a masque. It was the last time she was to see Darnley alive. At two o'clock that night a huge explosion rocked the city.

The noise was so loud that some citizens thought they'd heard cannon fire. Those who arrived on the scene first saw that the whole of the old Provost's house had been ripped apart and was now in ruins. Two dead bodies were soon discovered in the rubble but it was not until three hours later that Darnley and another servant called Taylor were found lying some sixty feet away in an orchard outside the town wall. Both were naked apart from their nightgowns and the king was under a pear tree, his hand draped across his genitals. Strangely there were no marks on him, or his servant, yet they were both quite clearly dead. Alongside Darnley was a cloak, a chair, a dagger and some rope.

Initial witnesses said that a group of men had been seen acting suspiciously near the house before the explosion and some neighbours claimed they had heard a man cry out plaintively, 'pity me kinsmen' in the early hours. The alarm was raised at Holyrood where the queen was said to be shocked, vowed to find the perpetrators and let it be known that she felt the murderers had aimed to kill her as well. Meanwhile, in the immediate aftermath of the explosion, members of the watch arrested a man lurking at the scene called William Blackadder, an associate of Bothwell. He claimed to have merely been drinking nearby and had come to see what all the commotion was about.

Ironically, it was Bothwell, the man who was to be most people's chief suspect for the murder, who began investigating the crime searching the scene and collecting evidence, though at one point he seems to have claimed that a thunderbolt had destroyed the house.

It was soon evident to everyone that a massive quantity of gunpowder had been used to blow it sky high. This had somehow been smuggled into the cellar or lower rooms of the house on the day of the murder, in which case Mary might well have had a lucky escape. Yet the lack of marks on Darnley's body suggested that he had almost certainly not died in the explosion itself. Instead, he had probably been smothered or strangled. The theory goes that Darnley woke in the middle of the night, disturbed by the noise of something untoward going on or had even seen shadowy figures smuggling gunpowder into the cellar. He had tried to flee the scene, perhaps using the chair and rope but been spotted and caught. One account claimed that Darnley was choked to death in a stable with a serviette in his mouth before being left under the tree.

In the days that followed, the Privy Council offered a reward of £2,000 for information that would lead them to the murderers. The citizens of

A sketch showing Kirk o' Field, where Lord Darnley was murdered. It was drawn in 1567 to help explain events to Elizabeth I. (Courtesy Wellcome Library, London)

Edinburgh, however, soon came to their own conclusion blaming Bothwell and even Mary, with placards erected across the city to that effect. When Elizabeth heard the news of Darnley's death, she wrote to Mary warning her cousin not to 'look through your fingers' in pursuing those responsible, in an echo of Maitland's words about Moray.

Claims from Lord Lennox, Darnley's father, that Bothwell was indeed to blame eventually pressured Mary into allowing a specially convened trial that April. The shambolic proceedings saw Bothwell turn up with 200 supporters. No proper evidence was submitted and Lennox was stopped from attending. Unsurprisingly Bothwell was acquitted.

Bothwell now launched his own audacious bid for power, organising a new bond at an Edinburgh tavern where he encouraged many of the nation's nobles to sign up to the idea that he should step in to the void and become Mary's husband. With breath-taking swagger, he next abducted Mary and took her to Dunbar Castle where it is claimed he raped her. Having hurriedly divorced his own wife, Bothwell returned with Mary to the capital and left many astonished when they were duly married on 15 May.

111

By now, however, Bothwell had overreached himself. Many of his former allies including Maitland and Morton turned against him. An army was raised, carrying banners that featured the dead body of Darnley himself and at Carberry Hill on 15 June, Mary was taken prisoner, while Bothwell escaped, going into exile. The queen was forced to abdicate in favour of her son and despite escaping imprisonment soon ended up fleeing to England.

This rapid turn of events had rather obscured the question of just who had murdered Darnley. A selection of Bothwell's henchmen were arrested, but their depositions, perhaps extracted under torture, were often contradictory and only tended to muddy the picture of what had actually happened at Kirk o' Field. The first to be found guilty, despite his protestations of innocence was Blackadder, hanged drawn and quartered in June 1567, with various body parts sent to towns across Scotland for prominent display. In January 1568, William Powrie, the man alleged to have masterminded the bringing of the gunpowder up to Kirk o' Field went to the gallows. Three other men, George Dalgleish, John Hepburn and John Hay were also sentenced to death. Hay implicated Bothwell and another servant, Nicholas Haubert, who stated that Bothwell had revealed to him the plot to kill Darnley in the days before the murder. Haubert said that he had actually delivered the keys of the house in question to Bothwell. Haubert was executed in August 1569 and another of Bothwell's associates, known as Black Ormiston, was put to death in 1573. Just how the gunpowder got into the house or where exactly it came from remains a puzzle. Whose was the dagger? What we can be certain about is that the plot was rather poorly conceived and did not quite go according to plan.

Bothwell was an aggressive individual, prone to outbursts of violence and it seems easy to assume that he was, at least in part, responsible. He may well have been part of a wider conspiracy involving the likes of Morton, who later became regent. Morton was executed in 1581 after he was eventually found guilty of being involved in Darnley's murder and in his confession said that Bothwell was one of the chief planners of the crime. By this time the truth had become shrouded in claim and counter-claim and accusations of being involved were being used as a convenient tool by whichever faction was prevailing politically to try and vanquish their opponents. Thus Archibald Douglas, who supposedly left his shoe at the scene of the crime, was tried but then acquitted while his servant was found guilty and executed. Balfour was also accused and acquitted.

The truth is that Darnley had no shortage of enemies; there were plenty of people who wanted him dead. The so called Craigmillar Bond, which Mary claimed to have seen, might have proved their complicity but, had it ever existed as an actual document, it was almost certainly destroyed in order to protect its signatories upon her capture.

There have been countless theories about what happened on the night of Darnley's death and even a wild idea that Darnley had actually meant to blow up the queen using the gunpowder and accidentally blown up himself instead. The biggest question that has faced historians is the degree to which Mary might have been involved in her husband's murder. The accusation gained weight with the 'discovery' of the so called Casket Letters. These were made public by Moray, who had slipped out of Scotland after Darnley's murder and returned to become regent after Mary's abdication. The letters were alleged to demonstrate a love affair between Bothwell and Mary that predated Darnley's murder. In one missive she is supposed to have said: 'Cursed be this poxy fellow that troubleth me this much.' Many people believe the Casket letters to have been forged or tampered with. Even if they are not genuine, Mary may still have lured Darnley back to Edinburgh and, knowing he was to be murdered, lodged him separately, so he could be efficiently dealt with by others who shared an interest in seeing him dead. On 9 February, Mary had conveniently left Darnley just before the building was blown up. One account even has her dressing in men's clothing so she could creep back out of the palace and watch the murder unfold. On the other hand, maybe Mary just wanted to bring Darnley back to Edinburgh to stop him working up a rebellion of his own and may have, as she herself pointed out, only just avoided death by the skin of her teeth. Mary is unlikely to have shed too many tears at Darnley's death and even seen it as sweet justice for what happened to Riccio. Yet it seems, rather than being directly involved, she simply turned a blind eye to the scheming of Bothwell and other nobles.

If Mary had been instrumental in the removal of Darnley it certainly didn't help her secure her throne as she might have hoped. Instead, his death plunged her reign into a desperate downward spiral. In 1568, both Bothwell (in his absence) and Mary, now a prisoner in England, faced investigation by Elizabeth's government for Darnley's murder, with the Casket Letters produced in evidence. Bothwell died in prison in Denmark

James VI of Scotland, later James I of England, as a child praying for his murdered father in a propaganda painting intending to show Queen Mary as the villain. Engraving by George Vertue, after *The Memorial of Lord Darnley*, Livinus de Vogelaare, 1567. (Courtesy Wellcome Library, London)

while judgement on Mary was simply suspended. She was kept in custody for the next eighteen years. Then, on 8 February 1587, she was executed at Fotheringhay Castle, having been found guilty of plotting to kill Elizabeth. By this time, following the tenure of four separate regents, her son James VI had taken up the reins of power in Scotland. In time he would, of course, become king of England too, escaping the kind of 'gunpowder treason and plot' to which his father had succumbed when Guy Fawkes' bid to blow up the English Parliament was foiled in 1605.

Chapter 15

Strangled with a Towel
1570

The tiny village of Spott lies in a lonely part of the Scottish lowlands, a few miles from the coastal port of Dunbar and a stone's throw from the Great North Road as it curls through the undulating countryside between Berwick and Edinburgh. Its parish church has a solitary air, standing aloof from the rest of the settlement; the graveyard boasting dramatic views over wide fields and out over the sea far beyond. But on a chill day the ambience here seems to chime with the darker side of the village's history which includes several bloody battles between the English and the Scots. Between the late sixteenth century and the 1720s the area was also gripped by the witch finding frenzy and between 1593 and 1705 some seventy-three people locally were brought to trial charged with the crime. Few were acquitted. Today, lying by the roadside just south of Spott, is a potent reminder of the location's gruesome past. The Witches Stone, a rough rock surrounded by railings, marks the place where one condemned witch, Marion Lillie, was burned to death in 1698. Her offence, it transpires, amounted to not much more than frightening a pregnant woman.

By the time this superstitious fervour was sweeping the locality Spott already had a reputation for more earthly criminal matters. In 1543 a former parson from the village, Robert Galbraith, who had gone on to become a judge in Edinburgh, was murdered by John Carkettle in revenge, it was alleged, for showing favouritism in a suit which had come before him. In 1570, a subsequent parson ended up in the frame for murder, but this time the crime was committed much closer to home.

A member of the new Presbyterian Church, which had been established following the Scottish Reformation, John Kello was a man who came from humble origins in Linlithgow, but had worked his way up through the church with plenty of study and determination. He was already married when he became the rector at Spott. His wife, Margaret

Thomson, had borne him three children and Kello became popular locally. Yet it seems he had rapidly become dissatisfied with his lot in life, seeing both his financial situation and humble spouse as stumbling blocks to furthering his career. Not content to rely on his meagre parson's stipend, Kello invested much of his money in property, winding up in debt when his purchases failed to deliver the hoped-for returns. At this point, Kello began to ruminate that if he were to find a new wife, one with the right connections, he might better himself after all. His eye fell upon the single daughter of the local laird. Kello would later say that what motivated him was the 'continwall suggestione of the wicked spreit to advance myself father and farther in the world.' Slowly, the scheming churchman began to make his plans. First, he was careful to make a will in his wife's favour to make it look as if he expected to die first. Then, cruelly, he began to spread gentle gossip about Margaret's unsettled state of mind.

It took Kello some time to pluck up the courage to act out his murderous fantasies. And when he did so, he opted to try and poison his wife. But Margaret merely vomited up whatever substance he hoped would do away with her, thanks, it was said, to the 'cleannes of hir stommocke'. The callous Kello needed a new plan.

On the morning of the 24 September, 1570, Kello was giving a sermon in his church, or 'kirk'. It impressed his congregation with its oratory and passion – a performance that was evidently somewhat more spirited than usual. The exact facts of what happened next differ depending on what account of the case is being followed. One, set down in the sixteenth century *Historie of King James the Sext*, by an unknown author, has it that, after the service, Kello brought some of his neighbours back to his house for some refreshments. When the party got there they found the front door locked. Kello cried out for Margaret to let them in. When she didn't appear Kello led the group to the back door and let himself in. In the Reverend John Thomson's version of the tale, given in the 1836 *Statistical Account of Scotland*, Kello had gone from the kirk after the service and asked a neighbour if, as his wife was feeling low, she would come and share dinner with them. On returning to the house they found the door and windows barricaded.

The accounts agree that once inside, Kello made a show of looking for his wife, before finding her in a bedchamber dangling by the neck from a rope. She was already dead. Feigning grief Kello then cried out, 'My wife, my wife, my beloved wife is gone!'

As far as the local community was concerned, Margaret had committed suicide. After all, hadn't her husband spoken of her private torments before? Now a bereaved single father, Kello was the recipient of their heartfelt sympathies. It seemed that, after a suitable period of mourning, Kello would now be free to go and make the new, 'better' marriage that he sought.

But Kello had made a mistake. It turned out that before his wife's death he had, at some point, fallen sick. During his illness he had been attended by another man of the cloth, Andrew Simpson, from Dunbar. At this time Kello had told Simpson about a fevered dream he'd had, in which he was carried off by a 'grym man before the face of an terrible judge,' but had escaped, despite being pursued by angels wielding swords.

Following Margaret's death it seems that Simpson became suspicious. He remembered Kello's dream and believed, in retrospect, that it was a sign of a guilty mind. When, a few days after her death, Kello came to see Simpson, no doubt hoping to be comforted over the loss of his wife, his fellow clergyman instead accused him of being the author of a 'crwell murther' and urged Kello to confess his crime. Kello finally admitted it was true. Briefly, he considered fleeing the country yet concluded that while an escape would be possible, he would never be able to outrun his own troubled conscience.

After careful consideration Kello made his way to Edinburgh. Once in the city he sought out a judge and some clergymen, admitting to them that he had, indeed, murdered his wife. He told them how, on the morning of the fateful day, he had crept into Margaret's chamber while she was at prayer. Quickly grabbing a towel, probably the nearest thing to hand, he had then strangled her. Margaret did not, it seems, die immediately. According to Kello's florid confession, made from his prison cell, Margaret had time for a few last words in which she managed to tell her husband she bore him no ill will and was glad to go to her grave if her death could do Kello 'vantage or pleasure'. Once the poor woman had expired Kello put a rope around Margaret's neck and strung up her body from a hook in the ceiling, making it look as if she had hanged herself. Here he had left her, then made his way to the front door and locked it, leaving the key inside, heading out of the building via a back exit. Kello had then made his way to the church where he calmly undertook his parish duties as if nothing untoward had happened.

Once Kello had unburdened himself to the authorities judgement came

117

swiftly. It was decreed that Kello be hanged for Margaret's 'crewell and odious murthure' and his body burned. On 4 October he was brought to the scaffold, where he expressed his contrition to the assembled crowd. He told them that if he had his time again he would cherish his wife. He also countered rumours that he was a witch. 'I have never,' he maintained, engaged in the 'wicked practices of the Magiciens'.

Perhaps his candour was not altogether in vain. Usually in such cases the property of the condemned felon would be forfeited. However, in this case, Kello's property was not confiscated in its entirety as we are told that some provision was made for his son Bartilmo and his daughters Barbara and Bessie.

So, is there any doubt as to Kello's guilt of the pre-meditated murder of his poor wife? In his account of the case in *Twelve Scottish Trials*, William Roughead briefly puts forward the notion that Kello was, perhaps, not guilty at all. Did his wife indeed do away with herself and could his subsequent behaviour be explained by a disturbed mind? Why the sudden attack of remorse? Roughead speedily dismissed his own postulation, concluding that the weight of evidence, as it existed, was against Kello. Nothing further seems to have arisen in the last century which would challenge his confident assertion that Kello must have been 'guilty of his wife's blood.'

Chapter 16

The Curious Case of the Corpse in a Cask
1572

In the early morning of 29 April, 1572, a mysterious large vat, which had arrived by boat, was opened on the harbourside in the town of Rye in Sussex. As the lid was prised off in the gloom, the body of a dead man spilled out. He had been badly mutilated and it was clear that the death was suspicious. But who was this stranger and who had killed him?

In Elizabethan England investigations of crime could be slapdash, depending on the sometimes unreliable efforts of parish constables, coroners and justices of the peace. But in the case of Rye's 'corpse in a cask' there is an example of careful detective work and effective co-operation between the authorities in different localities leading to a successful prosecution for murder. It reveals that Tudor justice could not only be swift but that a dangerous criminal could be pursued and caught with a level of skill which would be impressive even for modern professional law enforcement organisations.

The body in the vat had been brought to Rye by a local mariner, John Julians, but it was quickly clear that he had no knowledge of the dead body he had been unwittingly transporting from London. The corpse had been found at 4am, suggesting that Julians and his boat had only recently arrived in the town and also that there had been some kind of tip-off. An inquest was quickly convened and on 30 May the body was formally examined by the coroner. It was found to have three shallow wounds on the skull. There was lots of bruising too. The injuries were consistent with having been hit over the head. The man's throat had also been cut and he had a wound in the left side of his body which was judged to have been inflicted by a dagger or sword. Revealing just how gruesomely thorough these inquests could be the official record notes that the inquirers could not find the 'bottom of it'. Adding to the list of injuries, one of the victim's legs had been severed below the knee, cutting it almost clean off.

The jurors, led by George Raynoldes, deputy mayor and coroner, testified that they could not identify the man. He was not, it seemed, local. However there was one man present who did know him. He was a 'messenger' who had recently arrived from London and was no doubt the person who had raised the alarm with the local authorities about the presence of the dead body in the innocuous-looking vat. He was able to quickly tell the coroner that the dead man was Arthur Hall, a successful London merchant who had been cruelly murdered earlier that year. The inquest's verdict was as follows: 'We fynd that Artar Hall, that John Jyllyns broght home frome London ded in a drye pype, was mordred in the hed wyth three wounds, hys throt koot and throst in the left syde, hys left leg koot of bye the kne and hong bye the scyne the last daye of Apryl.'

A letter in the archives, dated 1 May, from the recorder William Fleetwood (the most senior judge in London) and the city sheriff John Branch, thanked the Rye mayor and his men for their efforts in the matter and told them that after Hall's wounds had been meticulously logged they were free to bury the body. On the morning of 2 May, Hall's remains were placed in a coffin and buried in one of the chancels of St Mary's, the 900-year old parish church. The same letter from Fleetwood told the mayor of Rye that he could also release the messenger who had been told by its burghers not to leave the town.

It turned out that by the time Julians' boat had divulged its bloody cargo, the authorities in London already had their prime suspect for Hall's murder in custody – a man called Martin Bullocke. Indeed he had, according to Fleetwood and Branch, already confessed to the crime. Bullocke had been arrested at the Red Lion inn, at High Holborn, which would then have been just outside the city walls. Before that he had been on the run.

Bullocke had been born at 'Barwike', which could have been Berwick-upon-Tweed, but there are several other places called Barwick scattered across the country and so his exact origins remain unknown. Nor do we know what Bullocke's profession was as such. But we do know that during 1572 he had access to the parsonage of St Martin's Outwich, a church which was located in the city of London on the corner of today's Threadneedle Street and Bishopsgate. In the sixteenth century it was already 200 years old and known as St Martin With the Well And Two Buckets, for its location near an important urban water source.

Bullocke was evidently something of a wheeler dealer and in his 1577 account Holinshed tells us that he arranged to meet Hall at the parsonage with the promise of buying from him 'certeine plate.' In the Tudor era gold and silver plate was highly prized and a marker of someone's wealth and status. Hall arrived to view the wares but was suspicious of the provenance, finally saying to Bullocke: 'This is none of your plate, it hath Doctor Gardeners marke and I know it to be his.' Bullocke retorted that indeed Hall was correct but that Dr Gardener, 'hath appointed me to sell it.' This was obviously a lie and it seems that Bullocke was now worried that Hall would bring his theft to light.

Holinshed picks up the story: 'After this talke, whilest the said Arthur was weieng the plate, the same Martine fetcht out of the kitchin a thicke washing beetle and comming behind him stroke the said Arthur on the head, that he felled him with the first stroke; and then strake him againe, and after tooke the said Arthurs dagger, and sticked him, and with his knife cut his throte.' A washing beetle was a kind of wooden bat used to beat laundry and would have made a formidable weapon, being heavy enough to inflict the serious wounds to Hall's skull.

Following his savage and sudden attack Bullocke had the problem of what to do with the body. He needed to come up with a plan to dispose of his victim's body fast, before the crime was discovered. At first he found a chest and tried to bundle the body inside. It was too short. Bullocke decided to try and bury Hall in the building's cellar but the winding stairs made it impossible for him to get the body down.

Bulllocke then grabbed a hatchet and proceeded to try and cut Hall's legs off, finally thrusting his body into a 'drie vat' and trussing it up with straw. Bullocke now planned to get the evidence as far away from him as possible. He arranged for the vat to be collected and taken to a ship, saying that it contained merely his 'apparell and bookes.' We have no idea why Bullocke paid for it to be sent to Rye, but perhaps he hoped that by the time the body was found it would be so far away that it could not be connected back to him.

Despite his attempts to dispose of the body after Hall's disappearance suspicion soon fell on Bullocke, presumably as people knew Hall had been on his way to see him. Bullocke was questioned by the alderman and Branch. But Bullocke was obviously clever enough not to incriminate himself. Branch could find no firm evidence against him, or as Holinshed puts it: 'so small likelihood appeared that he should be guiltie.' In fact, Bullocke was so good at feigning innocence that a local clothworker called Robert Gee, living in the parish of St Laurence Pountney, took pity on him and gave him surety. Gee, 'supposing the offendor to be cleere in the matter, undertooke for his foorth coming.'

But Bullocke didn't hang around, fearing that the law might catch up with him if he stayed in London. Holinshed says that Bullocke 'slipt awaie, first to Westminster', then on to Kingston finally holding up at Wokingham near Windsor'

Meanwhile, the suspect having absconded, poor Gee had been put in gaol. However, from captivity, with the sanction of Branch, he was allowed to send out servants looking for Bullocke. One of these was sent to Rye. It was, we assume, the messenger referred to in the recorder's letter. What neither Holinshed, nor any of the other records show, is how Gee knew about the vat aboard the ship and how it had arrived in Rye. It seems as if Branch and Fleetwood had been canny in getting a man like Gee, who now had the motivation that his own freedom was in peril, to do their detective work for them. More 'police' work, based on information and rumour, must have been involved in tracking Bullocke down to the Red Lion. He'd no doubt returned to the capital thinking enough time had passed for him to be able to reappear in the city.

Bullocke was found guilty of murder at the Newgate sessions on 22 May with the help of the information supplied from the inquest at Rye. He was hanged on a gibbet, at the 'well with two buckets' in Bishopsgate on 24 May. It was, Holinshed says, 'due punishment for his heinous and most wicked offense.'

Chapter 17

A Lust that Led to Double Murder
1573

George Browne was obsessed with Anne Saunders. He would later admit that he could not resist 'the appetites and lustes of his sinfull flesh.' And one chronicler tells us that he was desperate to marry Anne 'whome he seemed to love excessively.' Another describes him as 'addicted to the voluptuousnesse of this vaine world.' Sadly for George, Anne was already married to another man, also named George. She had wed the merchant tailor George Saunders in around 1560 at Harefield in Middlesex and by 1573 the couple already had 'manie children' together. A wealthy man, Saunders was related to some of the leading dignitaries of the time. He was, for example, the cousin of Sir Edward Saunders, Chief Justice of the Queen's Bench, while his wife, born Anne Newdigate, was also from a family that boasted good connections. These were important people in Elizabethan society.

Little of Browne's background is known, though there are indications that he was an army captain and came originally from Ireland. He also seems to have had some connections at court. Intriguingly, his brother Anthony achieved notoriety after being hanged in York for some 'notable felonies'. It's probable that Browne fell for Anne Saunders after seeing her at the house of a friend and widow called Anne Drewry, (referred to as Anne Calfield in official records) and then orchestrated matters so that he dropped in to visit her at the Saunders' home, in London's Billingsgate, while her husband was away.

The main facts of what happened next have down come to us from Elizabethan translator Arthur Golding in his work *A briefe discourse of the late murther of master George Saunders* written shortly after the events. It alleges that George Saunders himself did not know Browne. What remains unclear is whether Anne was as infatuated with Browne as he was with her. There is certainly no convincing evidence that she and

Browne had actually engaged in sexual relations. Yet there is no doubt that Browne was consumed with a real passion for Anne. In fact he was so determined to be with her that he resolved to murder her husband. Drewry, for her part, encouraged the enterprise and promised to help pave the way for a marriage to Anne once Saunders was out of the way.

On Tuesday 24 March, 1573, Browne received a letter from Drewry informing him that on that very evening Saunders would be lodging at the home of a Mr Barnes in Woolwich. The next day he would be making his way on foot to St Mary Cray, a village that lay to the south in Kent. What business he had there is not known.

By seven o'clock on the morning of Wednesday, 25 March Browne was lying in wait in the thick undergrowth, near Shooter's Hill – already infamous as a place frequented by brigands who preyed on wealthy travellers. Soon, he saw Saunders coming towards him. He also observed, perhaps with surprise, that there was another man accompanying his quarry. This was John Beane, a servant of Mr Barnes. Both Saunders and Beane were, no doubt, armed. But Browne caught them by surprise, attacking with his sword drawn, rushing upon Saunders and running him through. Golding tells us that Saunders was 'striken quite and cleane through at the first blowe.' Falling to his knees he just had time to ask for God's mercy before collapsing, dead. Realising he could not leave a witness Browne attacked Beane too, leaving him mortally wounded, and then fled.

Despite suffering 'ten or eleven wounds' Beane was still just about alive and managed to crawl away from the scene until he was, according to the chronicler John Stow, found by an old man and his daughter and taken back to Woolwich. Here Beane was able to give the authorities a description of Browne.

Meanwhile Browne was reeling from the shock of what he had done. Golding says that he was 'striken with suche a terrour and agonie of hart', that he 'coulde brooke nother meate nor drink' for the rest of the day. He seems to have been rather at a loss as to what he should do next. Golding says that first he sent a message via Roger Clement (also known as Trusty Roger and in official records of the time as Roger Symes), a servant of Anne Drewry, telling her that he had carried out the killing as planned. Presumably, Trusty Roger had been stationed near to the scene of the murder waiting for instructions. Stow reports that Browne's next move was to make his way to Greenwich, where Elizabeth was holding court and where he could hide among the multitude of hangers on. Soon news of the murder arrived in Greenwich and Browne now decided to head for Drewry's house in London, which was probably not part of the original plan. It is likely she realised the danger because she refused to see him herself, sending Browne away again and dispatching Trusty Roger to give him £20. Clearly she thought it best for the killer to lie low somewhere until the coast was clear.

At this point in the story there are some unfortunate unknowns. What, for instance did Browne do with his murder weapon? Why exactly did he go to Greenwich, only to leave again? More importantly, how did suspicion fall upon Browne, for it certainly did and very quickly. As soon as the day after the murder, the Council at Greenwich issued 'A letter to the mayor of London to cause diligent inquiry to be made for a murdre donne the day before upon one Saunders, an honest merchaunt man, one Browne being vehemently suspected.' It may have been that in the course of the day Browne had been observed acting oddly and that was why he moved on to London. Perhaps somebody in Saunders's circle or family were aware of his affections for Anne and suggested his likely involvement.

Drewry herself was also quick to learn that Browne was now a wanted man and Trusty Roger again came to Browne – wherever he was hiding – giving him more money and advising him to take flight abroad. At first he refused, presumably because he knew this meant an end to his hopes for a union with Anne. He must have been persuaded in the end, because by the Saturday he was at a relative's house in Rochester, Kent, seeking passage out of England on a ship to Holland. His pursuers might easily have guessed that he would take this route. Golding relates that the Privy Council ordered 'so speedie and narrow searche to be made for hym in all places,' that Rochester's mayor, acting on information that Browne was on his patch, quickly went to the house where the wanted man was lodging. Browne was promptly brought back to Woolwich where he was identified by John Beane. The culprit's apprehension hadn't come a moment too soon. After naming Browne as the man who had attacked himself and Saunders, Beane died just two days later.

Browne was then taken to Greenwich where he was questioned by the Privy Council, which had shown itself unusually interested in the case. On 1 April, Browne was thrown into the Tower of London where he eventually confessed, perhaps under torture. Strict instructions were issued for his incarceration there. He was not, the orders said, to be allowed to see anyone, though interestingly, friends of Saunders were to be allowed in to witness the questioning, suggesting they had some useful knowledge of Browne's intimacy with Anne Saunders. Browne duly confessed and must have revealed that his motive in attacking had not been robbery, but love. He implicated Anne Drewry as his accomplice in the killing, admitting that he had 'oftentymes before pretended and soughte to do the same, by the instigation of the said widowe'. This suggests it was not the first plot they had devised and suggests that any relationship with Anne might have been long standing. In his *A View of Sundry Examples*, published in 1580, the chronicler Anthony Munday states as a fact that Anne had consented to the murder and was therefore also an accomplice. But if Browne had been tortured there was one thing he refused to confess under duress. He vehemently denied that Anne knew anything about the conspiracy to murder her husband. She was, he maintained, not 'privie or consentyng' to the slaughter.

Arraigned on 17 April at the Queen's Bench in Westminster, Browne admitted his guilt. Three days later he was brought to Smithfield to be hanged. Even on the scaffold he took the opportunity to reiterate – in front of the massed crowds – that the object of his affections was innocent. Browne not only denied that Anne had been involved in the murder but also refuted the idea that they had enjoyed carnal relations. Stow says he 'laboured by all meanes to cleare mistres Saunders of committing evill of her body with him'. Was he telling the truth, given that he now had nothing to lose, or was his simply trying to protect the woman he loved? Once he had been hanged, Browne's body was hung in chains at Shooter's Hill.

In the meantime, Anne Drewry and Trusty Roger had been brought in for questioning. In his confession Roger implicated Anne Saunders, but when the authorities approached her they discovered that she was pregnant. The wheels of justice were now brought to a halt, but not for long. As soon as Anne had been delivered of her baby she 'was upon mistresse Druries man's confession, and other great likelihoods, likewise committed to the Tower.'

The trial of Drewry and Anne Saunders took place on Wednesday 6 May at the Guildhall where they both pleaded not guilty. The case against them was that they had, by letter, procured the murder, knew that it had been done and then helped the murderer financially. They were accessories before and after the fact. Trusty Roger was brought in to give his evidence against Anne who made a 'stoute deniall.' Nevertheless the jury found both her and Drewry guilty.

If Trusty Roger had thought helping the prosecution would see him win a reprieve he was sorely mistaken. On 8 May he himself was arraigned at Newgate and condemned as an accessory to murder. He was also found guilty and told he was to be put to death on the same day as his mistress. The execution date was set for the 9 May. However, the trio's execution was delayed for four days on the basis that George Saunders' account book, showing his financial transactions, had not been found. The real reason was so that the authorities could extract a confession from Anne. This was important as a warning to others and to help maintain faith in the system of justice. She was still stubbornly refusing to admit her guilt. And perhaps what happened next had something to do with a bid to blacken her name, proving to the public that the correct verdict had been made in a controversial, much debated, case.

The bizarre twist to the story was that a minister called George Mell had been allowed into Anne Saunders' cell at Newgate prison, where she had been taken after the trial. He had been given the job of offering spiritual guidance to the prisoner. In effect, he was expected to encourage Anne to make a full confession to the murder. But Mell had failed to stick to the script. Instead he had become convinced of her innocence. Some chroniclers say that he had even fallen in love with Anne himself. Golding tells us that the pair came up with a cunning plan to get her pardoned. Directed by Saunders, Mell went in to Drewry's cell and tried to convince the widow to take all the guilt on herself, so that Anne could be spared. Mell pointed out to Drewry that she was going to the gallows anyway and that if she saved Saunders a dowry would, in turn, be provided for her daughter's marriage. Eventually he persuaded Drewry to go along with it.

The ruse was apparently uncovered when Mell unwisely told another gentleman, who he thought was sympathetic, about the plan; he went straight to the authorities with what he had learned. When Mell came forward with his appeal, he was exposed and the pardon turned down. Mell himself was then committed to Newgate for his 'lewde practises with Saunder's wife.'

The ploy having failed, Anne Saunders was not yet prepared to give in. Overhearing some workmen talking about the strength of the gallows awaiting her she went to Drewry's cell herself and pleaded with her friend to stick to the plan and tell the authorities that she was not guilty. Drewry however was now more concerned with the state her own soul than in prolonging Anne's time on earth. She refused. Deflated, Anne Saunders now gave the authorities what they wanted, confessing her guilt in front of the Dean of St Paul's. She went further, admitting her 'unlawfull luste and liking of Browne'. When her husband's family were brought forth she contritely asked for their forgiveness.

Finally, on Wednesday 13 May, Saunders and Drewry were paraded through London to Smithfield on a cart. Golding tells us that a huge throng gathered along the route. 'For almoste the whole fielde, and all the way from Newgate, was as full of folke as coulde well stande one by another.' There were people hanging on to the gutters, sitting on tops of houses, clinging to the steeple of St Bartholemew's and even bashing down walls so that they could get a look.

By now Drewry had made her confession too, though at the Smithfield gallows she denied the rumours that she had dabbled in witchcraft or had poisoned her late husband. Trusty Roger also confessed. All three were then hanged simultaneously 'by drawing away the cart whereon they stoode.' Looking on from the pillory nearby was Mell who had been forced to endure the humiliating punishment for trying to tamper with the course of justice. He had a paper pinned on his chest which read: 'For practising to colour the detestable factes of George Saunders wife.'

Golding tells us that the case caused 'great occasion of talk among all sorts of men, not only here in the towne, but also farre abrode in the Countrie, and generally through the whole Realme.' There seems to have been open debate as to whether Anne Saunders really was guilty with some believing she was innocent or had 'brought hir selfe in danger of lawe through ignorance, and not through pretended malice.'

The case certainly caught the imagination of writers at the time. As well as Golding's report another pamphlet on the murder, called *A Cruell Murder Donne in Kent*, hit the streets in 1577. It was also given plenty of space in the chronicles of Holinshed and Stow. The crime was still remembered well enough in the 1590s that it became the basis of a play called *A Warning for Fair Women*.

On the basis of the evidence it might be concluded that Anne Saunders and George Browne had been engaging in an adulterous relationship for some time and even that Browne was the father of the child born prior to her execution, hence the urgency of the lovers to get rid of her husband. Drewry's motive would have been financial, getting a pay-out for arranging the killing. Yet there is a ring of truth in the absolute denial of both Browne and Saunders that Anne knew anything of the planned murder. Anne's latter-day confession in which she regretted her 'sinfulness of life' committed with Browne can probably be taken with a pinch of salt given the pressure she was under. It seems likely that while Saunders had known of or even indulged Browne's affections she had never expected him to murder her husband and merely felt guilty that any feelings she had shown him had led to such a tragic turn of events. In such instances, Tudor courts were primed to demonstrate that women were at the root of all evil. Yet there's no reason to doubt that Browne was the main driver in the horror that befell both George Saunders and John Beane.

Chapter 18

Murder Behind Bars
1581

Unlike many of those who were hanged for murder in the Tudor age, William Sherwood did not go to the gallows meekly or full of remorse. According to an account written shortly afterwards called *A True Report of the Late Horrible Murther Committed by William Sherwood*, he had not only perpetrated the crime of making speeches in defence of Popery, but had also shocked onlookers with his cowardice when he attempted to escape down the ladder and 'flye from the Butcher.' The hangman finally despatched him in the midst of treasonably reciting the Lord's Prayer in Latin.

Sherwood had fallen very far from the 'gentleman' who had originally hailed from the village of Walkington, a sleepy village near Beverley in Yorkshire. At some point he had fallen foul of the increasingly tough line taken against Catholics as Elizabeth's government looked to shore up the position of the still relatively infant Church of England. The recusancy laws meant those that did not confirm to the Protestant religion could be fined or put in prison and in 1581 these were tightened. Another law of *praemunire* made it an offence to assert the supremacy of a foreign power, which in practice meant the Pope. Sherwood, not uncommon for a Northerner, was a Catholic and it was for the offence of praemunire that, by the summer of 1581, he found himself incarcerated at the Queen's Bench, a prison in Southwark, London. He was also, the contemporary account tells us a, 'derider of God's ministers, a disturber of preachers,' and 'a contemner of the service confirmed by her majestie'.

There's a suggestion in the records that he had been there since 1577 and had later been ordered to serve perpetual imprisonment. Alongside him in the prison was another, apparently younger, man, of 'good parentage', called Richard Hobson. He came from the Isle of Wight and was also behind bars thanks to his alleged Papist leanings. From what we can tell of the way both were housed in the jail, their status meant that, rather than being simply thrown in a dank cell, they enjoyed reasonable comfort. But, a few weeks before being accused of murder, Sherwood had been moved to the 'common' part of the jail after finding himself in debt.

Money is often a motive for murder, but here the quarrel that led to Hobson's death certainly seemed trivial. It is likely that there was more to it than the surviving records show, but in the *True Report* Sherwood's urge to kill is put down to an unnatural thirst for blood brought on by popery. His vocal Catholicism was linked to the fact that he 'itched to commit murder.'

The well-meaning Hobson had struck up a friendship with Sherwood while in prison and now felt sorry for his indebted companion. He told Sherwood's creditors that he would cover the amount owing. When a friend sent Sherwood five pounds to cover the debts, Hobson got his hands on it (presumably because he was still in the better part of the prison). He then paid Sherwood's creditors with the cash directly, settling an outstanding sum from his own purse. Presumably this meant that Sherwood had been saved from languishing 'well shackled' in the incommodious section of the jail. Yet rather than take this courteous gesture in the spirit it was meant, Sherwood was furious with Hobson, feeling that he should have paid the five pounds to him directly on receipt. He began loudly sounding off about Hobson, protesting that he could not 'abide him'. Hobson tried to sort things out with Sherwood to no avail.

In fact Sherwood decided to take matters further. First, on the night before committing his crime, he made sure that Hobson wouldn not have anything about his person that could be used as a weapon with which to defend himself. Then, on 28 June, 1581, at about 8'o clock in the morning, Sherwood laid in wait for Hobson who had just finished his morning prayers. Sherwood, 'shutting his chamber door, assailed him with a knife and a stoole tressell, astonishing him,' and 'afterwardes gave him a large wound, keeping him downe and struggling till he bled to death.' Hobson had managed to cry out for aid from Master Throckmorton, one of the jailors. Hearing his pleas, Throckmorton and some others soon arrived to help. They broke down the door but were only in time to find Hobson 'soused in his own blood' and gasping for breath while uttering a few last, faint words. In the commotion Sherwood tried to make a dash for it, but he was quickly collared and brought before the marshal in charge of the prison, still covered in Hobson's blood. 'Being examined he denied the manifest murder, which by witness was proved'.

The case against Sherwood was heard at the assizes in Croydon, Surrey, where he pleaded not guilty to murder. He 'continued still obstinately denying the fact,' hoping for some 'helpe by pardon but a just judge prevented any ungracious hope.'

On 12 July, Sherwood was returned to Southwark, south of London, manacled during the journey to another condemned man who had been found guilty of rape. Sherwood's execution was scheduled for the following day and that night he was kept in the White Lion, a former inn situated on what is now Borough High Street which had been converted into a jail.

In his final hours, the pamphlet tells us, Sherwood's behaviour was 'resolute in opinion, driving off his Christian brethren that exhorted him, with dry scoffs'. As he climbed the ladder of the scaffold the next morning, which had been set up next to the Queen's Bench prison where the murder had been committed, Sherwood was determined not to renounce his Catholic faith or admit his crime despite being pressed to confess and make his peace with God. Instead he told onlookers, 'I beseech all Romish Catholicks to helpe me in this my extremetie with their vertuous and godly prayers for others which are of a contrary profession as I abhore their religion so I will none of their prayers. But if there shall be here present anyone of the true Catholic Romish faith, I beseech them of theyr prayers of my behalf.'

A cry rang out from the crowd: 'Hang him, hang him, there be none here by his profession.'

Of course, if there had been any present who shared his religious proclivities, they would have no doubt stayed sensibly quiet given the prevailing climate. Official records show that Sherwood was hanged for Hobson's murder, on July 13, 1581.

Chapter 19

Buried in the Cellar –
on New Year's Eve
1582

When, in the 1990s, the news emerged of the terrible crimes committed by serial killers Fred and Rose West, one of the most shocking aspects of the case was how many of the bodies of their victims had lain undiscovered, for many years, beneath the cellar of their home at 25, Cromwell Street in Gloucester. There is a chilling parallel in a case from the Tudor age which occurred in the year of 1582 in the town of Evesham, Worcestershire, just twenty miles away.

In the late sixteenth century, Evesham was a prosperous place, famous for the bounty of its orchards and a centre of local economic activity. It still boasts a number of impressive half-timbered buildings dating back to Tudor times and beyond, testimony to its historic prosperity. So it is perhaps no surprise that the story involves two local merchants or 'mercers'.

We learn from an anonymous pamphlet printed the following year that both of these mercers lived next door to each other in the town. Robert Greenoll, a bachelor, was the more successful, trading in 'all kindes of wares' and 'beloved' by locals for providing them with all their needs on market day. Thomas Smith, a handsome and newly married man, was the son of one of the leading figures in the town and also had a good reputation. Yet he found himself of 'indifferent welth'. Gradually he began to grow envious of his rival's business acumen and this jealousy led him to have dark thoughts. Smith became convinced that he should secretly kill and rob his rival. And so there were 'a thousand devises canvased over by this lewd man' as he formulated what he thought to be a fullproof plan of action.

While, technically, the new Tudor calendar began in March it was also still traditional to mark the beginning of the year, on 1 January, and also to give gifts at this time. So, on this particular New Year's Eve, Smith appeared to do the convivial thing of inviting Greenoll, who he knew to be a bachelor, into his house for some company and to share a quart of wine and some apples. Greeting his neighbour, he suggested that they, 'would passe away the evening pleasantly in friendlie talke and drinking together.' Greenoll, being a friendly type and keen to form a bond with a fellow trader, readily agreed to the idea and promised to visit later.

That crisp night the town was gripped with extra festive fervour, for a novel event was planned. A play was to be performed, perhaps at the surviving fifteenth century building that became known as the Booth Hall and may have once been an inn. As 'it drew towards night' the cry that a drama was to be enacted went up, 'whereto both old and young did hastily repair'.

The play provided the cover that Smith needed to enact his evil project. His wife seems to have been away and he hurriedly gave some money to the boy who usually helped him in his shop, sending him off to watch the performance as Greenoll arrived at the house. Smith invited his guest to sit down with him by the fire for a chat and a drink.

For a while Smith and Greenoll sat by the fire 'pleasauntly talking'. Then, Greenoll got up and stooped down to turn an apple in the fire. Seizing his chance Smith reached for a heavy 'iron pestell' that he had placed nearby. It was a tool which he usually used 'to beate his spice in the morters', but it now became his murder weapon. With his victim facing away from him, Smith suddenly gave Greenoll two 'mightie blows on the head'. Having crushed his skull Greenoll staggered backwards and fell on to the floor, 'yielding forth a verie pitiful and lamentable groane.' At this point we learn that Smith experienced a moment of regret for what he'd done, but quickly decided that Greenoll was beyond the point of recovery and what he had started he must now finish. Wielding his metal cudgel once more – a weapon likely to have inflicted grievous injuries – Smith rained down more blows on his victim. Although he was clearly dying, Greenoll's body was still 'trembling and shaking' and in some desperation Smith now grabbed a knife. He then attempted to cut Greenoll's throat but botched the job and then slashed at his body, only finding the shoulder blade. Finally Smith thrust his blade into Greenoll's heart.

With everyone at the play, Smith could be pretty sure that no-one had heard him carry out the killing or Greenoll's screams. He dragged the body downstairs into the cellar. Smith had already been down there earlier that day to dig out a shallow hole the length of a man and just deep enough to conceal a body and now entombed his neighbour. Then he smoothed over the makeshift grave with a plasterers trowel making the surface look as undisturbed as possible. He then showered flax over the floor and moved baskets and chests over the place where Greenoll was buried. Fetching some water Smith then washed the whole house from top to bottom aiming to get rid of any trace of blood.

Before he had buried the corpse, Smith had also gone through Greenoll's pockets to find his keys. Once his work in the cellar and house was done, he headed out into the night air, intending to let himself into Greenoll's property. Smith had clearly expected to find the street deserted but he had, perhaps, forgotten that at this time of year a nightwatchman was posted, who happened to be passing. Rattled, Smith blurted out the phrase, 'See and see not'.

The bemused nightwatchman continued to go about his business, but did not forget the exchange. Perhaps Smith thought himself such an important member of the community that the watchmen would turn a blind eye to theft. Boldly, Smith continued with his plan to let himself into Greenoll's store and proceeded to pilfer it, taking, 'a great deale of the goods from thence into his owne house.'

The next morning, the robbery of Greenoll's shop was reported by persons unknown. Greenoll himself was missing too. Initially, suspicion seems to have fallen on a stranger, particularly with the play in town. Actors weren't necessarily to be trusted and were almost certainly not local. But the watchman who had bumped into Smith that evening remembered what the mercer had said to him. He reported it to the town officials who also established that the last sighting of Greenoll had been at Smith's house. The mayor immediately asked for Smith to be found and brought before him, having a 'shrewd presumption against him to be somewhat faultie in the matter.'

Smith denied that there was any sinister meaning in his words to the watchman and claimed to be clueless about where Greenoll was. Unconvinced, the officials demanded to search Smith's house, but he claimed not to have the keys to the main house as his wife had them and was away in King's Norton, another village in Worcestershire. For some reason, however, Smith decided that he would let them look in the cellar,

The Booth Hall in Evesham which stood at the time of the murder of Robert Greenoll. (Copyright James Moore)

to which he did have the keys. Why did he make this dangerous offer? Perhaps, in his bravado, he felt he had done such a good job of burying the body that the officials could not find it. It was the obvious place to stuff the body if something untoward had happened to Greenoll, so perhaps if they did search the cellar and found nothing they would assume he was innocent and start looking for a culprit elsewhere. At any rate, Smith 'tooke the keyes from his girdle and threw them unto them.'

Those sent by the local bailiffs to search Smith's cellar found nothing at first but then one of them saw that a small piece of earth was disturbed by the stairs. On further examination the surface of the floor by the chests and baskets seemed softer. Removing the obstacles they began digging down. About seven inches beneath the surface, they made the horrible discovery of Greenoll's body and 'beheld how cruelly and unnaturally he had beene murdered.' Smith, who had been held elsewhere in custody while the search was undertaken, was now sent to Worcester gaol to wait for the assizes where he would face a charge of murder. We do not know the details of what happened at court, other than that he was found guilty and condemned to die by the judge.

Smith was duly hanged for the crime, but his relatives managed to successfully lobby that he was not gibbeted in a spot where all could reflect on his fate. This fact reveals that the law was open to influence. Yet the case as a whole also shows that justice was done despite Smith's connections. He had a 'father of good wealth and one of the chiefs in the towne'. Perhaps a trial was inevitable given Smith's cack-handed behaviour after he committed the murder. It's obvious that after the killing he had panicked, acting suspiciously with the watchman, making a hash of the robbery and telling obvious lies about not having the keys to his own house.

So what of his poor wife, who had been wed to Smith just two months before and herself came from a successful family? On her return from King's Norton the author tells us that she was full of 'greefe' when first she heard of this 'unhappy newes.'

Chapter 20

'Pressed to Death' for a
Cunning Crime
1589

In 1579 Sir John Conway was walking down a London street when a
fellow Warwickshire landowner, Lodowick Greville, sneaked up from
behind and, without warning, set about him with a cudgel. Conway fell
to the ground but Greville wasn't finished. He drew a sword and began
slashing at Conway with that weapon too. It was only because one of
Conway's servants intervened to ward off the blows that his master's legs
were not sliced clean off. Yet in the scuffle Greville did manage to 'hurte
him sumwhat on bothes his shynnes.' Greville was subsequently arrested
for the attack on Conway, who was actually a former friend and kinsman
through marriage and he soon appeared before the Star Chamber. We do
not know what motive Greville had for targeting Conway but he was
ordered to spend several months inside Marshalsea prison in Southwark
for the misdemeanour.

There is another, more shocking story, told of Greville in which he
appeared to joke about his own son's death. In 1560 Greville had married
Thomasine Petre, daughter of Sir William Petre, the high flying secretary
of state to four Tudor monarchs. At first the couple and their subsequent
children lived in Essex. While they were there, according to the tale, their
son Edward had been taking part in archery practice one day when, by
mistake, he fired an arrow straight up into the air. When it came down
the arrow pierced the body of his elder brother, killing him instantly.
Archery was one of the Tudor era's most dangerous pastimes; indeed, an
examination of coroners' records by historian Dr Steven Gunn, found that
it was to blame in at least fifty-six documented cases of accidental death.
Nevertheless, Greville's reaction was startling. It is alleged that he made
light of the matter, sarcastically taunting Edward by telling him it was

'the best shot he had ever shot in his life'. While the tale may be apocryphal there seems little doubt that Greville was a man possessed of a twisted mind and violent temper and years later, plagued by financial worries, his flawed character would lead him to plan a cunning murder.

Greville was from a wealthy family who owned estates in Gloucestershire and Warwickshire which he inherited at the age of just twenty-two. Vain as well as hot-tempered, he lavished huge sums of money on building a new house at his manor of Milcote near Stratford-on-Avon. Granted a licence in 1567, the pile was to be called grandly, Mountgrevell. In fact the house was never completed though the ruins of it were still visible as late as 1730.

In 1588, as the Spanish Armada threatened English shores, Greville managed to raise a body of cavalry to send to Tilbury where Elizabeth was raising an army to deal with any invasion. He almost certainly felt obliged to do so in order not to lose face because, well before this, Greville had been running seriously short of cash. He had already been in trouble with the courts for fraud and was in constant dispute with neighbours over property matters. Greville's answer to his money worries was to devise a dastardly plan to do away with one of his wealthy tenants.

According to the William Dugdale's seventeenth century account in *The Antiquities of Warwickshire*, Greville's chosen prey was a wealthy bachelor named Webb who was a tenant of one of his properties at Drayton in Oxfordshire. Making a show of generosity, Greville invited Webb to visit his residence at Sezincote in Gloucestershire for Christmas. During the stay, Greville selected two of his servants, Thomas Smith and Thomas Brock, to strangle his guest in his own bed, a task which they duly carried out. Brock was then persuaded to take Webb's place in the bed, impersonating him and pretending to be unwell by 'dolefully groaning'. Meanwhile, Greville called the local parson to attend on the patient and unwittingly witness the imposter agreeing to the details of a hastily drawn up will from his bed, complete with 'counterfeit voice'. The document granted much of the murdered man's lands to Greville. The 'sick' man was then allowed some rest and everyone was ushered out of the room. The corpse of Webb was reinstated and Dugdale says, 'News of his death was soon spread in the house, whereupon people were called up, who finding him dead in the bed took order for his burial.'

For some time it looked as if Greville would get away with the murder, but Brock could not keep the secret. After a heavy tavern session he boasted about what he'd done. As a contemporary account put it, 'One of the assassinates, being in his cups at Stratford, dropped out some words among his pot companions, that it lay within his power to hang his master.'

Hearing about Brock's indiscretion from Smith, the other murderer, Greville now took desperate measures. Dugdale says that 'to prevent the danger of any further such babling advised that he should be closely made away.' Smith did his bidding by drowning his fellow killer in a pit of water. But he was careless. Brock's body floated to the surface and was discovered. The local authorities soon identified Brock and found out that the person he had last been seen with was Smith, who was arrested. Smith spilled the beans on the whole conspiracy, naming Greville as the mastermind behind it.

Official records indicate that the victim was called Thomas Webb and that his will was made in 1585. He was not, as Dugdale asserted, a bachelor. In fact he had a wife by the name of Katherine. It was true, however, that he did make suspiciously large bequests to Greville. Dugdale is hazy on the timeframe of the murders, so it may be that Brock had kept quiet for a number of years before his loose lipped revelation that Greville was behind the killing. Interestingly, an alternative account of the case, related by Sir Thomas Coventry, suggests that Webb was poisoned rather than strangled but equally puts Greville in the frame.

Greville, along with Smith, was thrown in prison in January 1589. Because of his rank, Greville languished in the Tower of London for ten months before his trial as an accessory to murder. The case was to be heard at the superior court of the King's Bench instead of the local Warwick assizes. It was the murder of Brock, not Webb, for which Greville and Smith were to be prosecuted but this was probably merely because of a lack of evidence or concrete proof that Webb's will had been forged. When the proceedings were finally held on 6 November 1589, Greville endeavoured to exploit the law by refusing to enter a plea. He 'stood mute'. This meant that even though he might be found guilty Greville's lands could not be confiscated by the crown as was the usual custom. So, in saying nothing, Greville's son Edward would inherit, whatever his own fate. The punishment for not entering a plea was, however, grave. The court ordered that Greville should be executed using another ancient custom, 'peine forte et dure'. In other words he was to be 'pressed to death'. This involved the condemned individual having large rocks placed upon his body until the life had been crushed out of him (see page 19). It was certainly a much more painful way to go than death by hanging and showed that while Greville might be an unsavoury character he cared deeply about the future of his family line.

Accounts conflict as to where Greville's execution took place. Dugdale has it in Warwick, but in his *Annales of England,* written just three years afterwards, John Stow says it took place in London which seems more likely. Stow describes Greville being taken from the Tower of London on 1 November to Westminster for the trial, then to King's Bench prison in Southwark to be pressed to death on 14 November. According to Stow, Smith was hanged the same day at the Palace Court at Westminster.

Despite his sacrifice, Greville's direct descendants fared little better than the loathsome Lodowick. His son Edward may have retained his lands and was knighted, becoming an MP, but he was far from a popular man in Warwickshire. As lord of the manor at Stratford he regularly enraged locals especially over his attempts to enclose common land around the town. As such he carried on a protracted feud with Stratford's bailiff Richard Quiney, an acquaintance of the playwright William Shakespeare. It's believed that Edward Greville may even have orchestrated Quiney's murder in 1602. This upstanding local official was killed after doing his public duty one night by intervening to try and stop a drunken brawl. The affray was started by some of Greville's men, with the convenient outcome that one of the squire's biggest local enemies perished. Another local, Thomas Greene, wrote that Greville had 'his head grievously broken' by one of Greville's men.

However Edward Greville would go on to squander his fortune and ended up having to sell much of his land. His only son, John, died before him and this branch of the family died out. Some spoke of a curse on the Grevilles. In 1628, another related member of the family, Fulke Greville, seems to have fallen victim too. He was a famous poet and statesman elevated to the post of Chancellor of the Exchequer. But, in 1628, he was stabbed to death in Warwick Castle by one of his own servants, Ralph Heywood. The motive? A dispute over his master's will.

Chapter 21

The Bride who Poisoned Her Husband with Pancakes 1590

There are all sorts of reasons that lovers give for not wanting to have sex with their partners. Yet Anne Brewen's excuse for rejecting her new husband's advances must take some beating for novelty and bravado. Following their wedding night nuptials she refused to lie with her spouse, John, until 'he had gotten her a better house.' For good measure, Anne also told John that she was not going to give up her maiden name, Welles, until he could procure a befitting property and promptly took up lodgings elsewhere.

The truth was that the scheming Anne was not in love with her new goldsmith husband at all, but with another man in the same trade and together they now planned to do away with John as cunningly as they could. The subsequent murder was to become such a sensation of the age that it was recorded in a host of pamphlets and contemporary ballads. The most detailed account was given in *The Trueth of the Most Wicked and Secret Murthering of John Brewen*, which has sometimes been attributed to the celebrated Elizabethan playwright Thomas Kyd.

Anne Welles was a 'proper young woman' who was clearly perceived as quite a catch, for we are told that she had a 'comely personage' and was loved 'by divers young men.' One of these was bachelor John Brewen, an affluent London goldsmith who had become besotted with Anne and showered her with gifts of jewels and gold. He also enjoyed the favour of her 'friends and kinsfolk'. But there was another man called John Parker who was keen on Anne too. He was also a goldsmith but not free to marry, perhaps because he was not well off enough. Anne, no doubt flattered by Brewen's attentions and attracted by his prospects, accepted his gifts. Her real romantic feelings however were for Parker.

After a 'long and earnest suit' Brewen realised that he was making no progress with Anne, despite a 'promise between them'. Piqued, he asked for his gifts back. Perhaps Brewen had also got wind of rumours about a romance between Anne and Parker. After all, according to the pamphlet, the pair had already been intimate by this stage. In fact Anne was secretly pregnant with Parker's child. Anne then refused to return Brewen's presents. The furious goldsmith promptly had the woman arrested. We are told that Anne was 'astonished and dismayed' at the situation in which she now found herself. Yet she was so determined to keep her trinkets that she decided to reconsider her position. She told Brewen that if he would withdraw his action against her she would agree to marry him after all. Brewen was delighted and consented. It would turn out to be, in the words of the pamphleteer, 'the worst bargain that ever he made in his life.'

Parker, still consumed with passion for Anne, wasn't going to lie down and accept the situation. Despite Anne's agreement with Brewen it is likely she was still sleeping with Parker and after her marriage she made her home near his. He now began to urge her to do away with her husband. At first Anne rejected the notion, but Parker soon 'kindled such a hatred' in Anne's heart against her spouse that she agreed to kill him. Parker, on his part promised that once the murder was carried out he would marry Anne as soon as he could. They began to plot in earnest.

But how was the deed to be done? The couple had decided that poison would be the safest option. Anne didn't waste any time. Just three days into her marriage, on a Wednesday in February 1590, she put her plan into practice.

Parker had bought a strong, but unidentified, poison 'whose working was to make speedy haste to the heart without any swelling of the body' and gave it to Anne to put into Brewen's food. Despite not living in Brewen's house she arrived that cold morning with a 'plesaunt countenance' asking if it would please her husband to have a 'mess of suger soppes'. Sugar sops were a sort of Tudor pancake traditionally eaten in the run up to Lent. Brewen was pleased by the gesture saying, 'I take it very kindly that you will doe so much for me'. Anne then set about making the sugar sops putting some poison into the mixture. She managed to spill the first lot, so had to set about making up another portion, this time sending her husband out to get a snack of some herrings so she could concentrate on cooking and adding more of the deadly substance.

Brewen happily gobbled down the second lot of sugar sops.

Meanwhile Anne made a show of eating some from which the poison had been omitted. Within minutes the gulled goldsmith was racked with pain. He 'began to waxe very ill about the stomacke, feeling also a grievous gripping of his inward partes.' Pronouncing himself unwell, Brewen then proceeded to vomit violently, with 'such straines as if his lungs would burst in peeces'. He then asked Anne to put him to bed which she did. But when Brewen asked her to stay she told him she couldn't, returning to her lodgings, 'and so unnaturally left the poysoned man all alone that whole night longe, without either comfort or companie.' Brewen was sick all night, 'til his entrails were all shrunke and broken within him.' However it took the poor man nearly a week to die, with the fiendish Anne finally agreeing to attend on him after he complained that he was 'not long to continue in this world.' It seems Brewen went to his grave still not suspecting that his own wife was his killer. Brewen was buried on the Friday and no-one else appears to have suspected that his new bride might have had anything to do with his death either. His passing was put down to natural causes.

So Brewen's death was taken as an unfortunate, though not uncommon tragedy and when, some months later, Anne gave birth to a child everyone locally believed that the baby was his, not Parker's. The youngster sadly died in infancy. Meanwhile, during the next two years, Anne carried on her relationship with the 'lusty' Parker, who was a frequent visitor to her house. The pamphlet paints Anne as a pitiful figure who had become in thrall to him. Parker threatened to stab her with a dagger if she did not do as she was told and subjected her to continual physical abuse. The loathsome Parker, we are told, would 'haule and pull her as was pittie to behold.' Meanwhile he refused to marry Anne even when she fell pregnant with his child once more. Terrified that her reputation would be left in tatters Anne 'would not goe forth of her doors' fearing her neighbours would see her 'great bellie'.

However, the pair often argued and in one spat Parker refused Anne's exhortations to marry her, saying he would never wed such a 'strumpet' and accusing her of only wanting to get hitched so that she could poison him like she had done with Brewen. Anne shouted back, 'Why thou arrant beast, what did I then, why thou didst not provoke me to doo?' She continued, 'It had never been done but for thee: thou givest me the poison, and after thy direction I did minister it unto him and woe is mee ... it was for thy sake I did so cursed a deede.'

The trueth of the moſt wicked and ſecret murthering of Iohn Brewen, Goldſmith of London, committed by his owne wife, through the prouocation of one Iohn Parker whom ſhe loued: for which faſt ſhe was burned, and he hanged in Smithfield, on wedneſday, the 28 of Iune, 1592. two yeares after the murther was committed.

Imprinted at London for Iohn Kid, and are to be ſold by Edward White, dwelling at the little North doore of Paules, at the ſigne of the Gun. 1592.

Anne Brewen being burned at the stake, from the title page of a 1592 pamphlet *The Truth of the Most Wicked Murdering of John Brewen*. (Courtesy of Lambeth Palace Library)

Tudor dwellings had thin walls; people lived cheek by jowl, so it was no surprise that this row was overheard by some of those living close by. They reported what they had heard to the local magistrates. Anne was interrogated by Alderman Haward while Parker was quizzed by Justice Young. Both denied any knowledge of Brewen's murder. Then, the authorities played an old trick to trap them. Anne was made to believe that Parker had already 'betrayed the matter' and falling for the simple ploy she confessed, telling the whole story of what had happened. In the following weeks she was 'carried into the countrey' to be delivered of her child and afterwards brought back to prison.' Both Anne and Parker were brought before the sessions at Newgate in London in the summer of 1592. The pair were quickly found guilty of murder.

In his *Annales of England* John Stow told how in 'this moneth of June a young man was hanged in Smithfield and a woman burned, both for poisoning her husband, a goldsmith.' The sentence was carried out on Wednesday 28 June 1592. The court had specifically ordered that Anne should remain alive long enough to watch as Parker was hanged before she herself faced the flames of the pyre.

Chapter 22

The Man who Killed His Own Children for Money 1590

In the 1591 pamphlet entitled *Sundrye Strange and Inhumaine Murthers Lately Committed*, there is the brief tale of an unmarried 'young damsel' called Alice Shepheard, from Salisbury in Wiltshire, who denied being pregnant until it became impossible to refute it any longer. She revealed the truth to her mother and grandmother who fetched a midwife. Alice gave birth to a little boy. She then broke the neck of the child and, with the help of the other three women, secretly buried the body in the churchyard. Their crime would probably have gone undiscovered if a dog had not picked up the scent of the dead baby and unearthed it, exposing the corpse above ground. It was spotted by a passer-by, Hugh Mawdes, who alerted parish officials. Being a newborn baby and presumably with no record of a baptism or burial they quickly realised that this was a case of infanticide. Local folk, many of whom had surmised that Alice had been pregnant, suspected she was at fault. Her son's body was inspected at Our Lady Church in Salisbury by 'all the chiefs of the town' and Alice and the other women were examined by the local justices. Each swore, under oath that they had nothing to do with the child's death. However, on their way out of the building, one of the justice's servants overheard the midwife having misgivings about lying. All of the women were brought back in front of the justices and, eventually, all confessed to their part in the deed. They were put in prison and, at the next assizes, found guilty and sentenced to death.

Shame and duress, combined with worry about how she would provide for the child, were no doubt some of the factors that drove Alice to kill her own baby. In the same pamphlet, however, is the sorry tale of Nicholas Lincoln, a fifty-year-old man from Warehorne in Kent, who definitely did

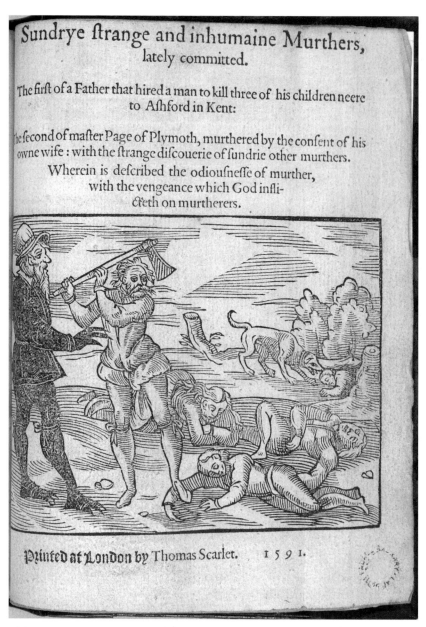

Sundrye ſtrange and inhumaine Murthers,
lately committed.

The firſt of a Father that hired a man to kill three of his children neere
to Aſhford in Kent:

The ſecond of maſter Page of Plymoth, murthered by the conſent of his
owne wife : with the ſtrange diſcouerie of ſundrie other murthers.
Wherein is deſcribed the odiouſneſſe of murther,
with the vengeance which God infli-
cteth on murtherers.

Printed at London by Thomas Scarlet.   1 5 9 1.

Title page of the 1591 pamphlet *Sundrye Strange and Inhumaine Murthers Lately
Committed.* (Courtesy of Lambeth Palace Library)

THE MAN WHO KILLED HIS OWN CHILDREN FOR MONEY

not love his children. Indeed he was prepared to take drastic action against them in pursuit of financial gain. Lincoln we are told, was a widow and the 'unnaturall father of foure unfortunate children' – three boys and a girl. A yeoman, we learn that he wasn't without means but had been seeking the hand in marriage of a wealthy widower. The woman refused him 'in respect of his great charge of children.' On learning this Lincoln was downcast and returned home, sitting down with 'great heavinesse' by the fireside. Another man, Thomas Hayton, who occasionally worked for Lincoln, happened to be at the house and seeing his employer looking heavy-hearted enquired why he looked so 'pensive'. Lincoln told him that his children stood in the way of finding a new, suitable wife. Then he blurted out: 'If I could make them awaie by any meanes I could marrie a rich widowe.'

The devil had 'entered so farre into his minde' that Lincoln had been considering just how he could make his children disappear. He was too much of a coward to kill them himself and now saw an opportunity. Here was Hayton, a poor labourer. Perhaps he could be bribed into helping. Lincoln offered Hayton forty shillings and a cow if he would kill his children for him. If, at any point Hayton should be suspected, then Lincoln said he would admit that he had been the culprit. At first Hayton hesitated, but 'as he was poor so he was covetous' and he finally agreed. The pair then set about planning how they could commit the crime and cover their tracks.

On the morning of 5 December, 1590 Lincoln had breakfast with his family as usual and then set off for the market in Ashford, a few miles away. He took his eldest son, aged fifteen and the labourer, Hayton, with him. At some point in the journey Hayton made an excuse and returned back the way he had come, leaving Lincoln and his son to continue on to town.

Once in Ashford, Lincoln bought three pairs of new shoes for his other children. It was all part of a sham. He knew that Hayton was already back at his house where he had 'speedily murthered,' the unsuspecting trio, 'knocking them on the heads with a hatchet and cutting all their throates.'

Lincoln sent his teenage child home from Ashford ahead of him while he did some more shopping. But when the son arrived at the front door he found it barred from the inside. He tried to raise the other children but could hear no sounds. Puzzled, he waited at the door for his father. When Lincoln came home he feigned concern and, rather than forcing his way

149

in or going to the back entrance as one might have expected, he went to get some of the other villagers to come to the house with him to help investigate what had happened. And so he 'came home with companie who were eye witnesses of this tragicall spectacle.' The villagers and the son were confronted by the bloody sight of two 'pretty' boys and a girl slaughtered, 'which grievous and unexpected sight made the beholders to stand amazed.' There was no sign of the murderer.

Despite his attempts to make it look as if his children had been the victims of an unknown attacker and create witnesses who could swear he had not been at the property at the time of the murder, Lincoln didn't do a good job of acting the devastated father. He 'made no signe of sorrow' and when the locals mentioned the name of Hayton, who had been seen around the property that day, Lincoln publicly dismissed the idea that he might be involved. Instead he commended Hayton as 'a verie honest fellow'. Then Lincoln revealed the full extent of his own callous nature. Incredibly he pointed the finger of blame at his remaining son.

In the next few days Lincoln began to behave very strangely. He 'would secke no meanes to burie the children nor that the coroner should view them.' Lincoln kept the corpses in the house for the next three days and kept everyone else away. A Mistress West was finally brave enough to call round to give him a ticking off for the ungodly way in which he was behaving.

Lincoln was now moved to bury the children. However, rather than having them taken to the churchyard, he took the bizarre course of digging a hole in his own house, burying all three of his victims two feet deep. News of what had happened had obviously got out as five days after the killings the coroner appeared on the scene. He found the children concealed under boards and just a little earth, swiftly ordering the bodies to be removed. In the meantime Hayton had been apprehended and arrested, though he denied any knowledge of the killings. The authorities seem to have ignored Lincoln's suggestion that his own son had been the murderer.

Hayton was brought before the bodies of the children. This was one of a number of cases where the corpses were said to have 'bled afresh' when confronted with their killer, thereby identifying him. This intervention by the Lord was, in practice, a convenient way to 'prove' guilt in the absence of witnesses or any other evidence. Hayton was said to have been so overcome with the sight that he confessed on the spot and went on to accuse the father too, revealing the details of the murder plot.

Both Hayton and Lincoln were taken to prison in Canterbury. The official record shows that they then appeared at the Sevenoaks assizes on 25 February and that, 'by inquisitions held on Dec 10th 1590,' a jury found that 'on Dec 5th Thomas Hayton from Hastings broke into the house of Nicholas Lincolne at Warehorne attacked the three children with an axe and then cut their throats with a knife.' Hayton pleaded guilty but Lincoln, indicted as an accessory to murder, refused to admit his part in the crime. He was nevertheless found guilty and he and Hayton were sentenced to be hanged. The execution took place on 27 February near Ashford, where Lincoln was finally induced to admit his responsibility for the 'foule and odious offence'.

Chapter 23

Murdered for 'Pulling Another Man's Nose' 1591

As he stood in the dock wearing a loose nightgown over a 'yellow frieze doublet' with his feet manacled and arms bound, Arnold Cosby must have cut an eccentric figure. Appearing at sessions held at St Margaret's Hill in Southwark on 25 January, 1591, the 33-year-old was accused of a dastardly murder. He had, the jury heard, callously killed an old rival, Lord Bourke. The contemporary chronicler John Stow logged that Cosby was charged with taking a dagger and subjecting Bourke to grievous injuries, 'of which mortall wound he died within two houres after.'

Both Cosby and Bourke hailed from backgrounds rooted in the torrid crucible of sixteenth century Irish politics. Cosby was born around 1558 at the family seat, Stradbally Abbey, in Ireland. His family has a well-documented lineage dating back to Saxon times and originally hailed from Nottinghamshire. His father, Francis, served as a soldier during the reign of Henry VIII. By the 1550s he had emigrated, taking up residence in the Pale, the part of Ireland under English control. Here he became involved in campaigns to extend power over other parts of the country and was frequently embroiled in tussles with the local Irish. In 1558, his efforts were rewarded by Queen Mary who made him 'general of the kern', heading a permanent fighting force, though in later years he would fall out with the crown over his corrupt dealings and conduct as a military commander. He also gained notoriety for his part in a massacre of seventy unarmed members of the O'More clan at Mullaghmast in 1578. He was to meet a bloody end in a battle of 1580, possibly with the collusion of some of his own men.

Perhaps a propensity to violence and duplicity was in the blood. Certainly Francis's son, Arnold, eagerly took up arms. He served, 'with great reputation' as a member of the Earl of Leicester's forces in the Low Countries during the 1580s, which were fighting alongside the Dutch against the Spanish. Cosby served at the Battle of Zutphen on 2 September 1586, where the poet Philip Sydney was killed. Made a captain, Cosby was soon given a pension of three shillings per day for his good service and by 1591 was said to be 'well known around court'.

John Bourke became the 2nd Baron of Castleconnell in 1584. It followed the ennoblement of his grandfather, Sir William Bourke, in 1580, a title granted to him by Elizabeth for his efforts in opposing a local uprising near their estates in the south west of Ireland. In the course of a skirmish with the rebellious James Fitzmaurice, John's father, Theobald, had been killed. But the Bourkes were victorious and Fitzmaurice's head ended up on a spike over the gate of Castleconnell.

By the 1590s both Crosby and Bourke had a relatively good pedigree within society, but there had been bad blood between them before the events of winter 1591. It's not known exactly what caused the quarrels but according to the chronicler Stow, Bourke and Cosby had already fought a duel at Greenwich and subsequently been 'made friendes'. But the mutual resentment seems to have festered.

At his trial Cosby would confess that things came to head when Lord Bourke had, one evening, 'pulled his nose'. Then, on 13 January, Bourke had received an insulting letter from Cosby in which he challenged him to another duel. As a peer, Burke's superior rank meant that he would have been well within his rights to deny Cosby the satisfaction of any such contest. But it's clear that Bourke now wanted to put an end to the affair.

Detailed accounts of what happened next have come down to us from several pamphlets, at least one of which appears to have been written by a servant of Lord Bourke himself. We learn from them that the duel took place at about 8 o'clock on the morning of 14 January in fields near Wandsworth, then in Surrey. No-one knows quite what happened next as the pair confronted each other alone, without 'seconds' as was usual in such duels. But it seems that before combat could ensue Cosby, who was described as 'a man of proude conceipte, borne of mischeiffe' feared that he might lose the contest, never having expected Bourke to accept his challenge. He therefore decided to play a contemptible trick on his foe.

Cosby first offered Bourke a choice of rapier, the weapons that were to decide their fate, making a show of measuring their length to prove that they were equally matched. We also learn that he then offered up the idea that they should both scar each other's faces and break the ends of their rapiers to make it appear to others as if they had fought. They could, he proposed, then call an end to the matter with their honour intact. Bourke wasn't happy with this suggestion insisting that they should fight. It was as this point that Cosby recommended to Bourke that if they were to duel he should take off his spurs, in case they impeded him. Bourke duly knelt down to do so.

His enemy now at a disadvantage, Cosby lunged forwards plunging his sword deep into Bourke's flesh, burying the blade a full 10-12 inches into either his foe's chest or shoulder depending on which report one follows. Then, grabbing a dagger, Cosby proceeded to inflict twenty-one to twenty-three more wounds upon Bourke's body in a frenzied attack. The doomed peer was left with injuries to his hands, arms and face as well as thighs, legs and even ankles.

Cosby then fled the scene, but his horse went lame a short time afterwards, hampering his escape. Meanwhile Bourke's footman had run to the house of John Powell, a man with the exotic title of Yeoman of the Bottles in the queen's household (which essentially meant he looked after the monarch's alcohol). The footman told Powell that his master and Cosby had gone out to fight on their own. Powell rode off in search of the feuding duo and discovered the bloody body of Bourke. He came across the peer being attended on by a female passer-by who was desperately trying to staunch the bleeding. Still alive, despite his extensive wounds, Bourke was taken by cart to a house in Wandsworth where, it was alleged, he lived just long enough to recount to the Earls of Essex and Ormond what had happened. Cosby was pursued and soon apprehended a few miles away in Newington. He was then examined and supposedly confessed to the murder, before being thrown into Marshalsea prison.

The case gripped London and there was a rush to publish pamphlets relating every detail of the sordid affair. The trial itself was attended by leading figures including the Lord Chamberlain, Earl Wormwood and Sir George Carey, Knight Marshal of England. John Popham, the Attorney General, prosecuted on behalf of the queen. Despite his earlier 'confession' Cosby now pleaded not guilty. He protested that, in fact, he had won the duel and having Lord Bourke at his mercy told him that he would spare his life if he would break his sword and return to the court, admitting that he had been in the wrong all along. He alleged that Bourke had refused. This evidence did not impress the jury and Cosby was swiftly found guilty. His request to be 'shot to death with bullets' rather than be hanged was denied.

On 27 January, Cosby was taken back to Wandsworth 'townes end' and a scaffold constructed near the spot where he had perpetrated the crime. According to a contemporary pamphlet he was now penitent, 'calling upon God to forgive him even to the last gasp.' Once hanged, Cosby's corpse was gibbeted for all to see.

The case leaves a number of intriguing questions unanswered. While Cosby may well have been sly enough to con Bourke into dropping his guard by the simple ploy of asking him to take off his spurs, is it unlikely that such an experienced soldier as Cosby did 'quaile' at the thought of death before the duel. Would he really rather have been 'at home' as one of the contemporary pamphlets asserts? As far as we can ascertain he was the man with the greater fighting prowess. Also, is it likely that a man who had suffered such a large number of wounds could have given a full account of what had transpired on that morning? However, if his injuries were as extensive as reported, it casts doubt on Cosby's weak claim that he was intending to spare Bourke as does the fact that he then left him for dead. Apart from Cosby's confession, almost certainly elicited under duress, we only have Bourke's word, transcribed by his own servant, that he had acted dishonourably during the duel. Cosby's lower status – a mere captain accused of killing a peer – put his defence at a disadvantage, especially with someone as esteemed as Popham presenting the case for the Crown. Certainly the long elegy attributed to Cosby, supposedly written in Marshalsea prison while awaiting execution was not written by him, but cast him as a Tudor ideal, the repentant villain, who realising his fate accepted God's punishment for his devilish deeds. Its final lines read:

That Cosbie hath misdone so hainously.
The circle of my time is compressed,
Arrived to the point where it began :
Worlde, countrie, kin and friends, farewell, farewell !
Flie thou my soule to heaven, the heaven of blisse !
O bodie ! bear the scourge of thine amisse.'

Chapter 24

Sir Francis Drake Investigates
1591

Best known as the man who had, in 1588, helped lead the English fleet to victory over the Spanish Armada, Sir Francis Drake had other, less celebrated, skills aside from his military flair. One of these was investigating crime on his home turf back in Devon. Drake, who was born in Tavistock, spent his early life as a buccaneer playing loose with the law, but in the 1580s he became an upstanding member of Devonshire society. He was made mayor of Plymouth in 1581, as well as a justice of the peace and subsequently Deputy Lord Lieutenant for the county overseeing the local judiciary. Drake had a keen interest in legal matters and personally gave money to the upkeep of Plymouth gaol. Over the next decade, when he wasn't on one of his acclaimed expeditions on the high seas, he could be found occupied with the more mundane tasks of ordering arrests and examining suspects in local cases concerning everything from petty theft to property disputes.

The most high profile case with which he was involved was the killing of Master Page of Plymouth. In February of 1591, he was on hand when Eulalia Page appeared before him and some of the other justices accused of orchestrating the murder of her husband. What emerged was a tale of thwarted love and a hopelessly bungled crime. It must have sparked Drake's interest more than most of the cases that came before him, as the accused woman was originally from Tavistock too. She was the daughter of Nicolas Glanfield, a wealthy shopkeeper in the town who left the day to day running of the place to a younger man from London called George Strangwich. Eulalia liked George and, given his abilities, her parents began to think that Strangwich, 'being a proper yong man', was good husband material.

The details of what happened next can be drawn from an account written in the same year as the events took place. In *A True Discourse of*

ACADEMIE DES SCIENCES,

280

MAR DE

oceanu

FRANCISCVS, DRAKE,

De, L'armessin, sculp,

Sir Francis Drake from an engraving by Nicolas de Larmessin, 1682. Drake helped investigate crimes in Devon during the latter 16th century. (Courtesy Wellcome Library, London)

a Cruel and Inhumaine Murder Committed upon M.Padge of Plymouth,
we learn that at first the Glanfields 'did wholye resolve' that Strangwich
should become Eulalia's husband, but that the devil now took an interest
in the dealings of these two young people. While it's not explicit that the
couple got a little too intimate for the liking of Eulalia's parents, this is
clearly the inference we are supposed to draw. They asked her to refrain
from Strangwich's company and hurriedly found 'a more meeter match'.
This was the ageing and miserly Master Page, a rich merchant from
Woolster Street who was keen to have an heir before he passed on. At any
rate, Mr Glanfield was planning to move to Plymouth and wanted his
daughter 'hard by.'

Eulalia's heart sank. The pamphlet tells us that 'she had settled her
affection altogether upon Strangwidge, yet through the perswasion of her
friendes though sore against her will, she was married to M.Padge of
Plimouth, notwithstanding that she had protested never to love ye man
with her hart.' Indeed, she vowed not to stop loving Strangwich and the
couple kept seeing each other when he made trips to Plymouth,
presumably on business. Neither found it a satisfactory arrangement and,
in desperation, they both talked of killing Page so that they could be
together.

Over the next year, Eulalia tried several times to poison her husband.
While he did 'vomit blood and much corruption,' which, the pamphlet
observes, would, 'doubtles in the end' have killed him, Eulalia grew
impatient as the potions she administered failed to have a deadly effect.
She and Strangwich now used some of their considerable financial
resources to bribe two other people into helping them take more direct
action. Eulalia gave one of her household's servants, Robert Priddis, some
money and promised a further £140 once he had done the deed. This was
a huge sum in Tudor England, more than a man like Priddis might earn
in a lifetime. It was enough to tempt him and he 'solemnly undertook and
vowed to performe the task.' Meanwhile, Strangwich managed to recruit
a man called Tom Stone to help with the murder promising him 'a great
summe of mony for perfourming the same'.

The pamphlet highlights that at this time Eulalia had recently given
birth to a stillborn child and, in her recovery, she had taken to a separate
chamber from her husband where, presumably, she could be attended on
by her maid. In fact we are told that Eulalia was by this stage already a
murderer, since she had done away with two of her own unborn children,

though how exactly she had achieved this is unclear. The pamphlet tells us that she'd done this because she did not want to have any children by Page – she had sworn 'she would never beare child of his getting.'

Eulalia's confinement gave her hired assassins freedom to target Page when he was vulnerable and alone in his own bed. On 11 February, at about 10 o'clock in the evening, Eulalia gave them the sign that the time was right. Stone and Priddis came to Page's room and crept in. But he wasn't soundly asleep and as the murderous duo edged towards his bed Page suddenly asked who had entered. Priddis leapt at him, but Page was awake enough to realise that he was under attack and sprang out of bed, on to his feet. He was stark naked, apart from a neckerchief. The pamphlet says Page would probably have overpowered Priddis if it wasn't for Stone who had managed to trip him up. With their victim now at their mercy on the floor both the attackers fell upon him. Grabbing the neckerchief they pulled it tight around Page's neck who desperately scratched at his throat trying to free himself. But, the pamphlet states, he could 'not prevaile, for they would not let slip their hold until he was full dead.' Unconscious, or already dead, Priddis and Stone now picked up Page's body and lay it across the bed, breaking his neck across the side of it. They then stretched out his corpse on the bed in a position as if he was still asleep, arranging his clothes as if he had just got undressed normally and merely passed away in his slumbers.

Next, Priddis went to Eulalia's bedroom to tell her that the murder was done. Then, an hour later, he came to her door again and cried out, 'Let some body look into my maisters chamber, me thinkes I hear him grone.' This was for the benefit of the rest of the Page household who were not in on the plot. Playing her part, Eulalia now pretended not to know what had happened, calling her maid – one of those who had no knowledge of the murder. She asked the maid to light a candle, put on a petticoat then went to her husband's door. Hesitating on the threshold she sent the maid in to look at Page first. For, the pamphlet tells us, Eulalia's 'conscience would not permit her to come and beholde the detestable deed she had procured.'

The maid went over and felt Page's face. She found it cold and his body stiff, then came out and told Eulalia who ordered her to put a warm cloth around her husband's feet making a show of thinking he was ill. But on applying the cloth the maid found Page's legs 'as cold as claye' and screamed out with the sudden realisation that he was dead. Eulalia sent her away to bed and then ordered Priddis to go and rouse her father, Mr Glanfield, who was, of course, now living in Plymouth. She also sent for a Mistress Harris, one of Page's sisters, along with a message. This was not that Page was dead, but rather that he was desperately sick and that she should hurry if she wanted to see her brother alive.

When Glanfield and Harris turned up at the house, Eulalia must have explained that it was too late and tried to act the part of the grieving widow. At first the visitors assumed that Page had died a natural death in his bed, as she had hoped. But Mistress Harris's suspicions were aroused when she spotted blood on her brother's chest, 'which he had with his nailes procured by scratching for the kercher when it was about his throate.' And when Page's head was moved she realised that his neck was broken. She also saw that the skin on his knees was grazed. With horror she grasped the fact that Page had been murdered and also had an idea of how it had been done.

With all haste, Harris now made her way out of the house and went immediately to the home of the mayor beseeching him 'to come and beholde this lamentable spectackle.' He rounded up some of the aldermen of the city and they all descended on the Page household. They quickly came to the same conclusion as Harris had done – that Page must have been 'murdered the same night.'

The conspiracy soon fell apart like a house of cards. Priddis was the first to be arrested and thrown in prison. There's no hint as to why suspicion fell upon him. Maybe he was the only other male still in the house and was thought to be the only one present physically capable of committing such a brutal act. Perhaps they found Page's blood on his clothes. It was certainly a sensible decision to bring him in. Once behind bars, Priddis quickly folded. On being examined he did 'impeach Tom Stone' alleging that he was the 'cheefe actor' in the killing.

The day after the murder happened to be Stone's wedding day. Remarkably he'd gone off to celebrate the nuptials just hours after helping to kill Page. But the investigators were not about to let a wedding party get in the way of making an arrest. We are told that 'being in the midst of all his jollety' he was seized and taken away to prison too. In turn, Stone implicated Eulalia who was also arrested.

It was at this point that Drake got involved. He, along with the mayor and other magistrates, examined Eulalia. She could not deny that she had plotted to kill her husband and said that she would rather 'dye with

Stangwidge, than to lie with Padge.' All three were held behind bars awaiting trial.

So what of Strangwich? A search was made of the city and he was found to be in Plymouth in the company of some men from London. Taken in, he confessed that he had been involved in the murder plot but had recently been having second thoughts and offered to prove that he had written a letter from London to Eulalia, advising that she and the others should not 'perfourme the act' after all. In the days following the murder the letter, a seriously incriminating document, must have been found, for the magistrates decided that since it had arrived after the murder Strangwich was still partly responsible and should join the others in being sent to Exeter jail to await the Lent assizes there.

Because plague was rife in Exeter at this time, the assizes were moved to Barnstaple in North Devon and it was here that Priddis, Stone, Strangwich and Eulalia were all found guilty of murder and sentenced to be hanged on 20 February. The town clerk of Barnstaple, Philip Wyot, kept a diary during the period and recorded that the gibbet was set up on the town's Castle Green. There were seventeen prisoners executed that day for various misdemeanours says Wyot, and four 'of Plymouth for a murder.' Priddis, Stone and Strangwich were hanged, while Eulalia was burned at the stake by default as she was guilty of petty treason, the offence constructed for women who had murdered their husbands and superiors (see page 18).

Just as they do today, crimes of passion involving young women attract plenty of comment and attention. Page's murder would attract the usual spate of ballads and, of particular note, a drama called *Page of Plymouth* published in 1599 and written by the famous playwrights Ben Jonson and Thomas Dekker.

Drake was soon off on maritime business once again, but he would shortly meet an end almost as undignified as the Plymouth murderers. He died from dysentery, in 1596, off the coast of Panama. The famous mariner was buried at sea in a lead coffin wearing a full suit of armour.

Chapter 25

Who Killed Christopher Marlowe?
1593

While William Shakespeare is, today, a household name across the globe the poet and playwright Christopher Marlowe, born in the same year as his fellow writer, is less well known. Possessed of a talent arguably equal to his Elizabethan counterpart, Marlowe's most famous work, *Doctor Faustus,* tells the story of a man who sells his soul to the Devil. It was the author's own double life, working in secret for the government while he penned the odd masterpiece, that has caused his sudden and violent death, at the age of just twenty-nine, to be shrouded in mystery and the subject of heated debate ever since.

'Kit' Marlowe worked his way up from a modest background. Born in 1564 at Canterbury in Kent he was the son of a shoemaker who shone from childhood, winning a scholarship to the King's School in the city and going on to study at Corpus Christi college, Cambridge. Over the centuries, he has earned a reputation as a hell-raiser. Certainly, as his literary career took off with the success of his great work *Tamburlaine the Great,* Marlowe seems to have followed a decidedly different and shadier path to Shakespeare.

We know for certain that from an early age he was in the queen's pay, probably having been recruited as a spy whilst a student and serving as part of the notorious intelligence network employed by Elizabeth's principal secretary, Sir Francis Walsingham. When, in 1587, there was some doubt raised by the college officials about the awarding of Marlowe's MA, due to long absences (as much as thirty two weeks in one year) a letter from the Privy Council was sent to the authorities at Cambridge insisting that the degree should be conferred in the light of his 'good service' to the queen and alluded to secret 'affaires' on 'matters touching the benefit of his country'. During the next decade Marlowe would turn up on the continent, almost certainly doing the government's bidding. His lavish spending habits also suggested that this was someone who had a source of income beyond that of a budding playwright.

Marlowe was a tough sort who never shied away from a punch up. In September 1589 he was living in Norton Folgate, part of Shoreditch in East London near the capital's main theatres. One afternoon Marlowe was found to be fighting in Hog Lane with a 26-year-old innkeeper's son, William Bradley. Marlowe's friend, the poet Thomas Watson, who'd had previous run-ins with Bradley, intervened, using his sword. Bradley died in the melee when Watson thrust his blade six inches into the other man's chest, killing him. Both Marlowe and Watson were initially arrested on suspicion of murder and thrown into Newgate prison. Marlowe soon got bail and was, that December, acquitted. Watson was soon released too. In May 1592 Marlowe would get into trouble with the law again, for assaulting two constables in Holywell lane.

A year later he would himself be a victim. Marlowe's grisly death, on 30 May, 1593, was as dramatic as anything in his plays. It has often been asserted that he was killed as the result of a tavern brawl arising from a trivial dispute. He was actually at a private house in Deptford, to the South East of London, run by a woman called Eleanor Bull, who hired the place out for meetings and meals. Here Marlowe had arranged to meet three other men at about 10am and spent most of the day in their company, dining, drinking, playing backgammon and walking in the garden. The official coroner's report, only unearthed in 1925, records that the others present were Robert Poley, Ingram Frizer and Nicholas Skeres. According to the inquest, that evening after supper, Marlowe was lying on a bed when there was some kind of dispute about the bill described, in the parlance of the day, as the 'recknynge'. Frizer was sitting at a table and facing away from Marlowe, wedged between the other two men. Erupting with fury Marlowe suddenly dashed at him. Snatching the dagger 'which was secured at his back' Marlowe then set about Frizer's head giving him two wounds. The men present would attest that in the ensuing scuffle Frizer somehow wrestled back the dagger from Marlowe and stabbed him over the right eye. According to the inquest Marlowe collapsed, dying instantly. Frizer's actions were deemed to have been in self-defence and he was soon pardoned. Marlowe's body was buried locally, just a day after his death.

The rudimentary nature of the official inquiry into the killing left many questions unanswered. Could Marlowe have been overpowered by Frizer on his own? As we have seen, this was a man who knew how to handle himself in a fight. Would he really have died so quickly from the wounds described? Medical experts doubt it. Many commentators have concluded that the inquest does not offer up satisfactory evidence that Marlowe's death was a case of self-defence and conclude that Marlowe was in fact murdered, with a whole host of different conspiracy theories arising as to what really happened and who ordered the killing.

The starting point for any notion that Marlowe's death was not an accident is the chequered characters of Marlowe's companions that day. Marlowe, we can be sure, had worked as a spy. And all three of the others had suspiciously shadowy backgrounds. Poley was a known government agent who worked as courier to destinations on the continent. He had also been a double agent who had helped thwart the Babington Plot, a scheme to assassinate Elizabeth in 1586. He once admitted that he would gladly perjure himself than say anything that would do him harm. Skeres was also a part time spy as well as a con-man and thief. Frizer was a servant, known for his dodgy dealings, in the employment of Thomas Walsingham, Marlowe's patron. If ever there was a trio capable of a murder and covering it up, this was it.

Also key to any murder theory are the mysterious events that led up to Marlowe's death. A year earlier Marlowe had been arrested over a counterfeiting scandal while in the Netherlands, accused by another shadowy figure called Richard Baines, with whom he was sharing lodgings. Baines was probably a spy too. It's possible that Marlowe may have been using the coinage to bribe Catholics for information. Interestingly no further action was taken against him in London.

On 12 May, 1593, Thomas Kyd, a fellow playwright and ex roommate of Marlowe's in London, had been arrested in an investigation into 'divers lewd and mutinous libels' which had been posted around London, some signed 'Tamburlaine'. Heretical tracts were found in his lodgings and under torture he had said that they belonged to Marlowe. There had, in fact, been growing rumours of Marlowe's supposed atheism. In late May a letter from his old enemy, Richard Baines, arrived at Court alleging that Marlowe had scorned God's word on many occasions.

By 18 May, 1593, a warrant had already been issued for Marlowe's arrest and two days later he attended the Privy Council for questioning. At this point he was bailed and merely told to attend upon them, regularly, until otherwise notified and not imprisoned. At the time Marlowe was staying with his literary patron Thomas Walsingham, the nephew of the deceased Sir Francis, at his home in Scadbury, Kent, possibly in an attempt to avoid the plague which had broken out again in London. Marlowe must have been a worried man at this stage. If proven, the charges of atheism and blasphemy could have seen him hanged, disembowelled whilst still alive and then drawn and quartered.

This series of events, quickly followed by Marlowe's demise on 30 May, have given rise to the idea that he was the target of a political assassination involving the powerful figures of the day who wanted to keep him quiet because he simply knew too much. If he was brought in for torture and trial he might divulge some of his many secrets. One theory involves Sir Walter Raleigh, who Marlowe is believed to have befriended. Raleigh was involved with the so called School of Night, a group dabbling with the ideas of atheism. Could Raleigh, or those close to him, have been worried that Marlowe, would expose them? Another idea links Skeres to the Earl of Essex, that favourite of Elizabeth, with the suggestion that he wanted to convince Marlowe to turn evidence against Raleigh. Other potential VIP culprits who have been forwarded include Lord Burghley, the Lord Treasurer; and his son Sir Robert Cecil, who are said to have been worried that Marlowe might expose their own heretical views. Eleanor Bull, the owner of the house where Marlowe died is thought to have been related, albeit it remotely, to Burghley. There have also been allegations that the inquest jurors and coroner could have been nobbled.

The problem with all these suggestions, apart from a lack of any convincing documentary evidence, is that ordering Marlowe's death in such a way was risky and surely done in a manner that was more complicated than necessary. Marlowe could have easily been dispatched less publicly.

There are some even wilder theories. There is the outlandish idea that Thomas's Walsingham's wife Audrey was jealous of the close relationship of her husband with Marlowe, who was possibly homosexual, and arranged the murder herself. Another suggests that Marlowe didn't die at all, and that he colluded with his fellow spies to fake his own death with his body substituted for another recently executed man. Some, who subscribe to this view, even propose that Marlowe was the true author of the plays attributed to Shakespeare. A staged murder seems an elaborate way for someone like Marlowe to disappear and simply too outlandish given the simple facts known.

Of course Marlowe might have been murdered in a simple row about money. Yet, even for someone who had a reputation for getting involved in sudden and fatal brawls it does seem simply too coincidental that Marlowe's death should occur at such a convenient moment, surrounded as he was by fellow masters of the dark arts of espionage. Their murky pasts beg the question as to why they were meeting with Marlowe that day. Perhaps these fellow spies themselves were worried about what Marlowe might reveal about them to the authorities. It is possible that they had spent the day looking for assurances from Marlowe but had already decided to kill him if they didn't get them. Poley, Skeres and Frizer could easily have acted alone and then simply agreed on a story and stuck to it when giving their evidence. The messy events of the 30th have all the hallmarks of a crime carried out by a small coterie of ruthless men, rather than an execution ordered from high profile figures.

Of course, we will never know for sure whether Marlowe was intentionally murdered or not. But we can be pretty certain that had he lived he would have gone on to create more great plays. Most of his works were published after his death and received critical acclaim. Had he continued to write he would surely now be a literary figure with the stature to rival Shakespeare in the public consciousness. Indeed the famous bard himself appeared to allude to the manner of Marlowe's death in his play *As You Like It*, written a few years later which includes the lines:

'When a man's verses cannot be understood, nor a man's good wit seconded with the forward child, understanding, it strikes a man more dead than a great reckoning in a little room.'

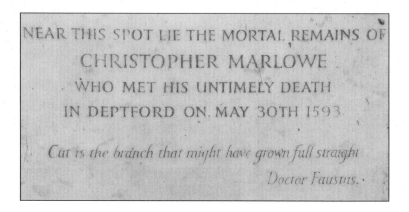

NEAR THIS SPOT LIE THE MORTAL REMAINS OF
CHRISTOPHER MARLOWE
WHO MET HIS UNTIMELY DEATH
IN DEPTFORD ON MAY 30TH 1593

Cut is the branch that might have grown full straight

Doctor Faustus.

Above: The church of St Nicholas', Deptford, the last resting place of the playwright, Christopher Marlowe, who suffered a sudden and mysterious death as reported by a plaque (left) in the graveyard. (Copyright James Moore)

167

Chapter 26

Death by Sex
1594

Across the centuries there have been many ways in which desperate husbands have murdered their wives. Few, however, have meticulously planned to carry out the fatal act during sexual intercourse. This was the method chosen by Thomas Robinson, a Tudor sailor and fisherman who lived in the ancient port of Rye in Sussex. A truly callous killer, he chose to subject his wife, Bridget, to a diabolical death as she, unwittingly, was comforting him with her warm embraces.

Robinson had apparently been a well-respected member of society until he got into debt due to his lavish spending. According to a version of the case told in a pamphlet of 1598, (in which his name is given as Henry Robson) the financially embarrassed fisherman was duly thrown into debtors' prison, 'where he long time remained languishing in woe'. The dutiful Bridget, however, did everything she could to help, aiming to earn enough to free her husband. Yet he saw only one way to escape from behind bars – selling all the couple's possessions and starting a new life. These items did not amount to very much: two beds; a cupboard; a table with bench and stools; three chests; a couple of spinning wheels and some lumber. They might, however, raise enough to pay off his debts. For some reason, Robinson saw Bridget as an impediment to achieving this goal. Perhaps she didn't wish to see their marital home dismantled. As time passed, Robinson became determined to make the task more straightforward by killing her. But just how was it to be done, so that no-one would suspect him?

Alongside him in prison was a man whose name was given in contemporary coroner's records as Humphrey. In the later pamphlet he is referred to as Glasier. In this account the fellow inmate sympathised with the fisherman telling him he was sorry to see such a beloved member of the local community locked up. The heartless lag merely replied, 'tis too late now to be sorie, when there is no remedie, for so long as my wife liveth, it is impossible that ever I should come out.' This led Glasier to reply, 'Faith then sure, if my wife's death could procure me libertie I would never be in bondage, or imprisoned.' Glasier, himself soon to be released from incarceration, then began to plot with Robinson how they would cunningly do away with Bridget. Together they would then quietly leave England for the Low Countries. The scheme they devised was both inventive and monstrous. When Glasier left jail he immediately went to a mercer in the town called Fisher and spent a penny on ratsbane (arsenic) often left out to kill rats. He went back to visit Robinson at the prison and gave him the package, telling his co-conspirator to mix it with some ground glass. Robinson did as directed and waited until one of his next meals, saving the skin from some shoulder of mutton and wrapping his deadly concoction – no bigger than the size of a hazelnut – inside.

Visitors were sometimes allowed into debtors' prisons and the next time that Bridget came to see her husband they had sex. Court records give the date as 26 May, 1594. In the pamphlet account, Robinson persuaded his wife to stay until morning by promising her 'the dearest night's pleasure that ever a woman had.' Evidently, in the dank darkness of his cell Robinson managed to secretly convey the package unseen and unfelt into her 'privie parts' while they were engaged in loving caresses. The inquest recorded that Robinson, 'did conveye into the boddy at her secret partes certeyen broken glasse and poison.'

From the pamphlet we learn that Bridget's body was soon swelling as the poison, 'began to runne and eate into her veins.' The pain was so great that she was confined to bed where she languished for five days. Nothing her neighbours, or several physicians who visited, could do helped her condition and the suspicion arose that her symptoms smacked of poison.

By 12 June Bridget had died, but the misgivings of those who tended her led to permission being sought for her body to be 'ripped'. At this post mortem the physicians apparently 'found in everie vaine both glasse and ratsbane and could not devise how or by what means it had come thither.' They did not think, however that she had been poisoned through her food or drink. A Tudor style murder inquiry was launched and inquiries were made around the town to discover who had recently bought ratsbane. Glasier's purchase at Fisher's quickly came to light and he was known to have been in prison with Robinson. Now suspicion fell upon

Bridget's husband, especially since it also came to the authorities' attention that he had slept with Bridget in the jail.

The pamphlet goes on to tell us that a Master Boulton examined Robinson and pretended that Glasier had spilled the beans on how he had planned to do away with his wife. But Robinson denied knowing anything about how she had died. Boulton told him, 'Nay if you be so obstinate, we will bring Glasier forth, who to your shame shall testifie it.' This was a ruse, as Glasier had already disappeared from the town without trace.

Under pressure Robinson at last admitted having had the ratsbane. At first he said he had wanted it to kill rats in the jailhouse, but eventually told Boulton, 'I have often heard that poison will breake open any iron lock, and therefore I bought it thinking thereby to get my libertie.'

Boulton replied, 'No thou hast not told the truth; for with it and glasse mingled together thou didst pyson thy wife; and therefore as thou lookest for any favour at our hands, confesse how and in what manner thou didst it and who was the counsellor of it.'

Robinson replied, 'Well then I perceive you glut after my blood and if it will pleasure you shall have it.'

The official inquest into Bridget's death was held the day after her death, 13 June, in front of Robert Bett, town mayor as well as coroner. The evidence here differs slightly from the pamphlet. One of the witnesses called was a man called Prescott who said he had seen Richard Sadler, the husband of Robinson's sister Jane, visiting the suspect at the prison in the days running up to Bridget's death. Brought before the jury, Sadler told how he had indeed bought a pennyworth of ratsbane from the 'Goodwyfe Fisher' but had given it to his wife to put down for rats. He had only been at the jail to take the prisoner some 'hose'. Re-examined after his wife gave evidence, Sadler admitted that his brother-in-law had actually asked him to buy the ratsbane for him when he had visited him in jail, giving him money to do so. Sadler said that Robinson had told him that he would use it to try and open the prison locks.

Then Robinson gave evidence stating that it was, in fact, Sadler who told him the ratsbane could open locks and that was why he gave Sadler 4d for the poison on 7 June. However, pushed by the court, Robinson appears to have come close to a confession. He admitted having had sexual intercourse with Bridget on 26 May and that Humphrey, (possibly Humphrey Glasier), who was imprisoned with him 'told him to poison his wife and made the glass and poison which killed her'. Evidently there was a second lot of ratsbane, from Sadler, which was never used. Robinson was perhaps concerned that the first dose had not worked, aiming to have a second attempt at murder when Bridget came to lay with him again. In fact, unknown to Robinson, the first lethal mixture was already taking its effect.

Robinson appeared in court at Rye on 17 June, where he pleaded not guilty to murder but was found to be responsible for Bridget's horrible end and sentenced to be hanged. He went to the scaffold on 19 June and was buried 'under the gallows'.

Although Rye is today a small, quaint tourist town, it was a busy place in Tudor times, important as one of the historic Cinque Ports and as a point for transporting troops to France. It had played a vital role during the defeat of the Spanish Armada in 1588 and would have been a melting pot of tradesmen and seafarers. Nevertheless such a heinous crime as Robinson's would have shocked the local inhabitants and the country as a whole, news of it evidently having spread far and wide.

Indeed the crime was so shocking in its savagery, even in its day, that the author of the The *Examination, Confession and Condemnation of Henry Robson* says that the like has not been known 'since Cain murthered the righteous Abel.' And while the author, known simply as L.B., may have embellished the case for literary purposes the existence of the original court records, bears out much of its detail.

Chapter 27

Denounced by His Own Son
1594

Ralph Mepham knew all about fire. It was his job to dig for iron ore in the mines around Mayfield in Sussex and 'make coals'. During the reign of Elizabeth, the village was at the centre of England's most important iron-making region and the industry was booming. Hundreds of men were employed to extract the ore, which would then be smelted with charcoal to make the metal at one of the scores of new blast furnaces which dotted the countryside. By the 1590s the region's iron industry was producing a massive 9,000 tons of iron per year, used in everything from nails to the navy's cannons. In the twenty-first century, Mayfield nestles in a rural, agricultural setting, but in Mepham's day it was a highly industrialized place full of noise and pollution with the brooding glow from the furnaces providing an eerie spectacle, both day and night.

In the late evening of 1 October, 1594, there was another blaze which lit up the sky in Mayfield. It was Ralph Mepham's own house burning to the ground. The threat of fire filled Tudor men and women with dread. With most houses made of wood and other combustibles, a house could go up in minutes, and spread to other buildings quickly too. It was second nature for neighbours to keep a watchful eye on anything that might seem amiss at nearby properties. So when another villager, Joan Baylie, saw flames leaping from the Mepham house that night she cried out for help and ran to see what she could do. She believed both Ralph and his wife, also called Joan, to be out but that the couple's five-year-old son was inside. Running into the house with some of her other neighbours to save the boy who was 'like to perish' she came across him still alive and hurried the youngster out of the property. The villagers then tried to salvage what goods they could from the burning house, but in the end the flames beat them back. It was only later that they found the charred body of Joan amid the burning embers. Yet it soon became clear that she had not died from the blaze or smoke inhalation. Her throat had been cut.

The parish constable was called for. He was a man described in a 1595 pamphlet as 'very honest', but it was unlikely that he had ever encountered anything so serious and at first he couldn't 'tell what course to take to find the murtherer.' The pamphlet (in which Ralph's surname is given as Deaphon) says that a coroner's inquisition was immediately opened and that Joan Baylie was sent for 'to finde what they coulde of the death of the woman'. But Joan had no more useful information. It was at this point that the surviving son, who was also called Ralph, was brought before the inquest and asked, by the coroner Magnus Fowle, to tell what he knew of the night's terrible events. In *A Most Horrible and Detestable Murder* we are told that 'the boy without any blushing feare tolde them that his father came home when his mother was a bed and first used some churlish speech unto her, then he drew out his knife.' Ralph must have been sleeping in the same room as his mother for he was able to tell the court that next, without apparently hesitating for a moment, his father 'cut her throat and left her to die.' Despite his youth and the fact that he must surely have been traumatised by the death of his mother, Ralph junior was able to give the court a detailed description of the murder weapon, 'describing in good order the bignes of the knife' and even the colour of the handle. Given that his father was still alive, Ralph junior was either very brave or too young to understand the repercussions of the evidence he gave.

The pamphlet tells us that as soon as he had committed the murder, Ralph senior had calmly left the house leaving Joan bleeding to death or, as the anonymous author puts it: 'weltering in her owne goare'. After the killing, the miner simply went back to work 'without making any semblance of sorrow for this most odious murder.' The fire that followed seems simply too coincidental to have been an accident, though the pamphlet tells us only that 'leaving some candle or fire in such place of danger that the house therewith was fired.' He may have knocked over a candle during his frenzy. More likely, Mepham had used one to set fire to the house, presumably with the intention of burning to death both Joan and his only son, so that he could not reveal what had happened. Yet the blaze had not destroyed the evidence as he had hoped, for his good neighbours had run to 'quench it'.

Having survived, Ralph junior's testimony was now seen as crucial.

Quizzed by the coroner as to his father's motive for the crime, the five-year-old could not offer any explanation. The pamphlet says: 'Wherefore his father did this wicked deede hee coulde not say anything.'

Once the boy had given his evidence, the court ordered that Ralph senior should be brought to them immediately from his work place. Then they 'strictly examined' him over the facts as they had been presented to them by his son. However Ralph senior 'stoutly and most audatiously denied the fact.' When asked where he had been whilst his house went up in flames, Mepham told the court that he had been at work the whole time. The coroner then asked to have a look at his knife, which Mepham duly pulled out of his pocket. It was observed that the blade was identical to the one that Ralph junior had described being 'in all points for bignes, colour … and all other markes', just as the child had earlier told the coroner. Mepham was then asked if the knife he had presented was actually owned by him. He told them that, in fact, it wasn't and that he had 'borrowed the same.' The poor son was brought forward again and asked if this were true. He refuted this telling the coroner that the knife did indeed belong to his father.

Now it was the turn of Mepham's workmates to come before the coroner and be questioned. They cast doubt on their colleague's story that he had been at work at the time when the murder was committed. They all agreed that at about five o'clock on the night of Joan's murder Mepham had left them. He had not returned to their mutual workplace until at least nine o'clock the same evening – after the fire had begun.

Their evidence, combined with Ralph junior's startling revelations, seemed damning, but it was not quite enough for the coroner, who decided that Mepham should be placed in the town stocks overnight, with the hope that the sanction might encourage the suspect to confess. Yet the pamphlet goes on to describe how, 'the next day being more thoroughly againe examined in the cause and the evidence being founde too apparent' Mepham still denied having done the deed. The coroner was, however, satisfied that there was enough evidence to have him indicted – as long as the boy testified.

The official record of the inquest, from 8 October, shows that Ralph was alleged to have 'murdered his wife Joan at Mayfield with a knife … which he held in his right hand, giving her a wound in the throat of which she died at Mayfield within an hour.' Mepham was taken to the jail at Lewes awaiting the next assizes.

On 24 February, 'with other notorious malefactours not unlike himselfe' Mepham's case was heard at the Grinstead assizes before Baron Robert Clarke and Serjeant Edward Drewe. Again Mepham's son was called to give evidence, with the prosecution's case largely resting on his testimony. He didn't let them down. The pamphlet relates how he told the jury exactly what he told the coroner in a clear, loud voice, 'which was in the child admired.' It was enough to see his father found guilty and Mepham was sentenced to be hanged. The execution was carried out on 27 February, 1595, at Grinstead with, as far as we know, Mepham still claiming to be innocent of the crime. No clear motive seems to have been identified, but it was probable, given his son's reaction that Mepham had subjected his wife to a long campaign of domestic violence and that, on one autumn night, he had finally lost all control.

What became of little Ralph the records do not tell us. The pamphlet concludes by warning: 'Thus God revealeth the wicked practices of men who thought the act be kept never so secret.' The court that convicted Mepham concerned itself with more mundane matters – carefully recording the value of the murder weapon as they always did. The knife used to kill Joan was said to have been worth two pence.

Chapter 28

The Murder that Inspired Romeo and Juliet 1594

In William Shakespeare's play *Romeo and Juliet*, a feud between the House of Montague and the House of Capulet leads to murder. At around the time it was written there was a real case of a feud between two leading families in Elizabethan England leading to a violent and controversial death. It was an incident of which Shakespeare would have been well aware and was almost certainly one of the bard's inspirations for the plot of his famous work.

The feud between the Danvers and the Longs, two of the most prestigious families in Wiltshire, dated back decades. Bloodfeuds were a relatively common feature of Tudor life and revenge killings were thought of, not so much as murder, but what the contemporary writer Francis Bacon called: 'a kind of wild justice.' Bacon thought that the law ought to weed out this contemptible behaviour. The reality was that if the families involved were important enough, those who oversaw the law in Elizabethan England might act leniently in such cases.

The very manner in which the Danvers family took up residence at the Wiltshire manor of Dauntsey set the tone for the bloodshed which would follow. At the end of the fifteenth century, the last heir to the manor there was a young man called Edward Stradling. In about 1488 he seems to have been murdered in a robbery along with his mother. Edward's sister, Anne, had inherited the manor and married into the Danvers family. By the 1590s Sir John Danvers was head of the family and had ten children, the most prominent of which were his eldest sons Charles, who served as an MP for Cirencester, and Henry, who became a soldier. The neighbouring Longs had been important landowners in Wiltshire since the twelfth century and had major estates at Draycot and South Wraxall. From 1581 Sir Walter Long, who evidently liked the high life, was the head of the family and a serving member of parliament. The wealth of both families meant that they kept on a large number of retainers, the very existence of which upped the ante when it came to disagreements.

It's not known exactly what caused the feud between these two great families but by the Elizabethan era the Danvers were linked to a faction that supported Robert Devereux, 2nd Earl of Essex, while the Longs had associations with Sir Walter Raleigh. Raleigh and Essex were at loggerheads during this period. It is likely, however, that more day to day issues were at the root of the tensions between the two families as they jostled for local dominance and that these eventually simmered over with tragic consequences.

Years of grudge and grievance would be brought to a dramatic crescendo on Friday 4 October, 1594. John Aubrey, the seventeenth century writer, stated that the very public killing that occurred on that day was planned at the parsonage in the village of Great Somerford, apparently with the connivance of the parson himself. Other accounts reveal that on the morning of the 4th Sir Charles and his brother Sir Henry, both then in their twenties, rode out together making for the town of Corsham to confront the Longs, accompanied by around eighteen hangers-on assembled in the 'most riotous manner'. It's clear that the Danvers knew just where to find their intended quarry that day.

There are conflicting accounts about what happened next, but the official coroner's record states that at about 12 o'clock, in the daytime, the Danvers burst into the house of one Chamberlayne, probably an inn, armed with swords and pistols. Here Sir Walter Long and his brother Henry were having a grand dinner. Seated at the table along with the Longs were many other gentlemen, including some of the justices of the peace of Wiltshire. If the Danvers had wanted to keep this confrontation a secret, then they had chosen the wrong venue.

According to the coroner's inquisition held the next day, Henry Danvers then 'voluntarily, feloneously and of malice prepense,' pulled out a small pistol and 'did discharge in and upon' the said Henry Long, 'a certain engine called a dagge, worth 6s 8d, with powder and bullet of lead.' The coroner, William Snelling, recorded that Danvers had been holding the gun in his right hand when he fired and inflicted 'a mortal wound upon the upper part of the body of Long under the left breast of which wound he instantly died.' Having killed Long the Danvers brothers immediately fled the scene. Long wasn't the only victim it seems. While his brother Walter had narrowly escaped death, a poor servant by the name of Barnard, who had simply been waiting at table, had also been killed in the commotion.

Whether either of the Danvers men really had planned to kill Long, or simply wanted to give him and his coterie a fright we shall never know. But following the coroner's inquisition they were immediately outlawed. Lady Barbara Long, Henry's mother, wrote to inform Queen Elizabeth 'of a verie strange outrage' and the Lords of the Council at the royal palace of Nonsuch in Surrey acted quickly sending an official order on 7 October to the High Sherriff of Wiltshire to 'apprehend so manie of those that were in this ryottus action as you maie by anie meanes have a notyce of, and to cause them to be comytted and straightlie examined concemynge the plott and purpose of this fowle attempt and murther.' A footboy called Henrie Bainton was specifically put on the wanted list as it was said that he had been sent in ahead of the killers to observe where everyone was sitting – adding weight to the idea that the murder had been premeditated.

Meanwhile the Danvers had been making good their escape. At '8 or nine o'clock' on the Saturday morning after the killing the Danvers arrived at the estate of their friend, the Earl of Southampton at Titchfield hoping for refuge. There's no direct evidence that the Earl knew the Danvers had been planning murder but he certainly helped them in their quest to avoid capture and was complicit in destroying evidence. He organised for the brothers to be hidden at a place called Whitely Lodge on his estate where they then laid up for a few days. A bloody shirt and saddle were spirited away by some of Southampton's servants. The Danvers were guided as far as Calshot Castle at the mouth of Southampton Water and subsequently smuggled out across the Channel to Calais before their pursuers could catch them.

Despite the findings of the inquest and the fact that the Danvers brothers were outlawed, no actual indictment for murder was ever brought against them, despite many eye witness accounts and potential testimony from those involved in getting them out of the country. As was often the case, those of high rank could bring considerable influence to bear. Sir John Danvers having died, his wife, Lady Elizabeth Danvers, began a long campaign to get her sons a pardon, including petitioning the Privy Council. In her account a very different version of the murder was presented, in which Sir Charles arrived to give Long several, 'blowes with a cudgel (without offring anie other weapon or violence) and being therewith satisfied offered to departe the chamber.' It went on to allege that Long had then attacked Charles Danvers, dangerously wounding him and that when Henry arrived to find his brother 'bleeding and fayntinge' he shot Long to prevent Charles' death. It seemed a rather contorted account and implied that everyone else who had been present at the dinner had been lying.

She also gave an alleged back story to the killing. Sir John Danvers, being a local magistrate, had committed a servant of Sir Walter for robbery but Sir Walter had intervened to 'rescue' him and had even himself been temporarily imprisoned for meddling in the course of justice. Danvers then committed some other servants of the Longs for murder and, in retaliation, Sir Walter provoked an affray in which one of the Danvers' servants was killed. Sir John's principal servant was also said to have been insulted by having a glass of beer thrown in his face. What really seems to have triggered the shooting was a series of letters Sir Charles Danvers had received from Henry Long. In one he threatened to whip him and had called him, 'ape, puppie, foole and boye'. The letters had been 'of such form as the heart of a man had rather die than endure'. Lady Danvers aimed to show that her sons had been driven by the Longs' continued insolence to seek a public reckoning. Furthermore, she went on to allege that since Long's death Sir Walter had sought to corrupt witnesses to his brother's murder and have hedges on the Danvers estate pulled down to boot.

Safely abroad, the Danvers brothers now entered the army of Henry IV, the French king. Two years after Henry Long's death they were lobbying to go home, hoping enough time had passed to be forgiven for the 'gentleman's quarrel'. On 3 October 1596, the Earl of Shrewsbury sent a letter from France to Sir Robert Cecil, one of Elizabeth's closest advisers, telling him, 'Heare is daily with me Sir Charles and Sir H. Davers, two discreet fine gentlemen, who cary themselves heare with great discretion, reputacion and respect.' He knew of the allegations against them but continued, 'God turne the eyes of her Majestic to incline unto them, agreable to her own naturall disposition, and I doubt not but they shall soon taste of her pittie and mercie.' It seems that by 1597, their attempts at rehabilitation were making good progress as Henry Danvers was accepted back into the English armed forces.

In 1598, Lady Danvers, clearly a formidable matriarch, made a new marriage to Sir Edmund Carey, who just happened to be a cousin of the queen. Soon all her efforts on behalf of her headstrong sons were rewarded. That June, Elizabeth decreed that both the Danvers should be pardoned, on the condition that they paid Sir Walter Long £1,500. By 1599, Sir Charles and Sir Henry were reported to be back on English shores, in London.

Charles' luck did not last long. Not content with having narrowly escaped the noose, he snubbed the monarch who had given him his pardon, joining the Earl of Essex's abortive rebellion against the crown in 1601. He was beheaded on 18 March at Tower Hill.

Henry Danvers, on the other hand, prospered. On his return to England he joined the army in Ireland, distinguishing himself and under James I he was restored as heir to his father's estates and made Baron Dauntsey. Later, in the reign of Charles I, he would garner more honours, being made Earl of Danby. The fact that he was officially an outlaw, despite his pardon and advancement, obviously stuck in his craw for some years. In 1604, he challenged the Corsham coroner's original findings with a 'writ of error'. This sought to overturn the decision to outlaw not on the basis that he was innocent, but merely on legal technicalities. He was successful and the coroner's judgement was found to be bad. Henry Danvers lived until the age of seventy, dying in 1643 and outliving his rival, Sir Walter Long, by thirty-three years. His burial in a 'great marble monument' at the church in Dauntsey is an unusual edifice for a man who had almost certainly killed a man in cold blood, but got away with it because he had the right connections.

On the very weekend that he had given the Danvers brothers protection, the Earl of Southampton was celebrating his twenty-first birthday and had held a feast at Titchfield. Some have suggested that William Shakespeare might have been present at this occasion, as Southampton was probably one of his patrons. More likely is that Shakespeare learned of the story from his friend, the Italian linguist John Florio, who was in the employ of Southampton and was involved in helping the Danvers get passage out of the country. This link has led many experts to see the story of Henry Long's death as an inspiration for Romeo and Juliet, a play which appeared the following year and tells the tale of two tragic lovers whose deaths bring about the end of a long running feud. In the play the action is given an Italian backdrop, but many aspects of the drama do seem to echo the real life Danvers and Long debacle. The feud between the Danvers and Longs mirrors the hatred of the Montague and Capulet families. There are the brawls between the servants of the two families, just like the spats between the Danvers and Longs retainers.

Long's murder has similarities with Tybalt's slaying in the play – at least the Danvers' version of it, which would have been the version that Shakespeare heard. Romeo's flight to Padua is an echo of the Danvers' escape to France. Then there is Lady Capulet, bent on revenge somewhat like Lady Danvers, who never gave up trying to get her sons off the hook. Of course, as with many stories about Shakespeare's sources, there is no absolute proof of the connection between this classic Elizabethan murder and Romeo and Juliet, but it seems to have more grounds than most. The Tudor historian A.L.Rowse was convinced that the parallels could not be put down to coincidence. He correctly pointed out that 'the affair made a sensation at the time' and concluded that, 'the Earl's poet was inspired by the theme of love and friendship, in the ambience of feud and death.' He merely gave the whole tale, 'an Italian setting, and wrote Romeo and Juliet.'

The magnificent marble tomb of Henry Danvers, the 1st Earl of Danby, at St. James the Great in Dauntsey, Wiltshire. A remarkable memorial for a murderer? (Copyright James Moore)

Chapter 29

Strangled for Beating His Wife 1600

The annals of the British Isles in the sixteenth century are peppered with examples of strong, fearless women, but they also indicate a society in which domestic violence was commonplace and one where some men treated their wives as mere chattels, to be physically beaten without fearing redress. Most of these female victims suffered in silence, though there are occasional glimpses from the records of what some had to endure. In the 1530s, Elizabeth Howard, Duchess of Norfolk, wrote to Thomas Cromwell about the abuse that she had been forced to suffer at the hands of her own husband, Thomas Howard, 3rd Duke of Norfolk. An immensely powerful man in the court of Henry VIII, the Duke was also notoriously cruel. Elizabeth claimed that as she had been recovering from the birth of her daughter Mary, he had grabbed her while she was still in bed, pulled her on to the floor and proceeded to drag her through the house by her hair. He had also wounded her in the head with a dagger. The Duke denied everything. He maintained, somewhat unconvincingly, that Elizabeth had got the new scar on her head from a surgeon in London – while he had been taking out two of her teeth. Norfolk was never made to answer for the treatment of his wife.

Some sixty years later a Scottish woman called Jean Kincaid also alleged that she had been the victim of a violent husband. While Elizabeth Howard had eventually moved out of Norfolk's home in order to escape his behaviour, Jean was driven to seek bloody revenge. Born Jean Livingston of Dunipace in 1579, she came from a prosperous family. Interestingly, her gentleman father, John Livingston, had got himself into plenty of trouble over the years and there is a suggestion that in 1595 he was implicated in the slaughter of a man called David Forrestier in a 'deidlie feud.' Despite his chequered past, by the turn of the century he was in such favour with the king, James VI, that he was attending on him at the royal palace of Holyrood.

Jean was just 15 or 16 years old in 1594, the year she was married to John Kincaid of Warriston. He was a considerably older man who may have been married before. Kincaid was also extremely wealthy, possessing a great deal of land around Edinburgh and was descended from the influential Kincaid clan originally from Stirlingshire. No doubt Kincaid's moneyed background was an attraction for Jean's family when they arranged her nuptials. Jean became known as Lady Warriston and took up residence at Kincaid's home, that 'gloomy house hanging over a deep black pool' which was located about a mile from Edinburgh. Over the next few years, Jean blossomed into a great beauty, at least according to the balladeers who would later chart the story of her sad life in verse. Married life with the laird, however, was anything but pretty. According to one account Kincaid subjected Jean to vile attacks, biting her arm and striking her 'divers times'. In one rage, at dinnertime, he threw a plate in Jean's face, splitting her lip. Some insight into the extent of the abuse comes from her later claim that 'Many dayes have I lived in this vail of misery.' Unsurprisingly, thanks to his terrifying outbursts, Jean 'conceived ane deadly rancour' against her spouse.

In the year 1600, Jean would have been just twenty-one, but she was already a mother with a young baby. She despaired of spending more years with the sadistic Kincaid, confiding to her nurse, Janet Murdo, that she felt like killing him. The nurse took up the idea and they agreed to find a man prepared to carry out the deed on Jean's behalf. Murdo said, 'I shall go and seek him and, if I find him not, I shall seek another and, if I get none, I shall do it myself.' The man they identified for the job was Robert Weir, a servant of Jean's father, who worked as a groom. There's little doubt that Jean already knew Weir. There may even have been some kind of romantic dalliance between them. Certainly she felt like she could count on him to save her from the monster she had married.

On 1 July, Murdo brought Weir to the house in secret to meet Jean and began feverishly plotting how to murder Kincaid. No time was then lost in executing their plan. Weir was hidden in a cellar until nightfall and, that evening, Jean made sure that her husband's wine glass was always kept topped up at dinner. Jean and Kincaid did not share a room and once her husband was safely asleep Jean crept down to get Weir up from the cellar. She led him to Kincaid's bedroom and they crept in. Kincaid began to stir but before he became fully conscious Weir ran over to the bed and began punching him, aiming for the jugular vein in his neck. He then continued to rain down more savage blows. Pulling his victim out of bed, Weir then began kicking Kincaid in the belly as he lay on the floor. Finally, to silence Kincaid's screams, Weir took Kincaid by the neck and strangled him. It was the kind of frenzied attack that suggested the perpetrator had as much hatred for Kincaid as had his wife.

Meanwhile, Lady Warriston had retreated to the hall, listening with horror to the 'pitifull and fearfull cryes' coming from her husband's room. Eventually they stopped and Weir emerged to inform her that Kincaid was dead. Jean pleaded with Weir to take her with him and flee from the city. He refused saying, 'You shall tarry still and, if this matter not come to light, you shall say he dyed in the gallery, and I shall return to my master's service … but if it be known I shall fly and take the crime on me; and none dare pursue you.' With that Weir disappeared.

Were John Kincaid's screams heard by others? Or did someone else discover his dead body before it could be disposed of? All we know is that officers of the law arrived on the scene shortly afterwards, finding the laird's dead body. They caught Lady Warriston 'red-handed' along with Murdo – the 'fause noursie'. At first, Jean attempted to play the grieving wife, but it seems her inability to pretend she was sorry for Kincaid's death may, in part, have given her away. She would later admit that she 'laboured to counterfeit weeping' … 'but do what I would, I could not find a tear.' Jean and the nurse were arrested and, along with two other servants, Barbara Barton and Agnes Johnston were placed in the city's Tolbooth prison.

On Thursday 3 July both Jean and Janet were found guilty of murdering Kincaid and sentenced to be strangled, then burned at the stake. What evidence was brought to prove their guilt we do not know but an eye-witness at the court said of Anne, 'it was a wonder to see how little she was moved in so far that when the sentence of death – that she should be hanged at a stock and afterwards burned to ashes – was pronounced against her, she never spoke one word, nor altered her countenance.' Barton and Johnston were acquitted, with Jean claiming they knew nothing of the crime.

During Jean's incarceration, a minister, the Reverend James Balfour, visited and asked her to repent for her crime. At first it had little effect. She raged at him saying: 'Pray for yourselves, and let me be'. Undaunted

Balfour spent the next thirty-seven hours trying to persuade Jean to seek God's mercy. Eventually she did consent to pray with him and, according to him, made her peace with the Lord. She was also allowed to see her baby son one last time, kissing him on the head and asking God to bless him.

Balfour later wrote an account of his time spent with Jean Kincaid and in *A memorial of the conversion of Jean Livingston* we also learn that she was not told the hour at which she was to be executed, but while she waited she could hear the crowds baying for her blood from outside in the streets. Jean also confessed that although she had been afraid of facing trial for the murder, she indicated that she had hoped that her father's position at court might have got her some kind of pardon.

In fact Jean's father and relatives seemed to have simply wanted to save their own repuations, lobbying to get the embarrassing Jean out of the way as quietly and quickly as possible. None of them visited her while she was waiting to be executed and, if any plea for mercy was made, it fell on deaf ears, though her sentence was reduced from burning to beheading. Her death was scheduled for the early hours of the morning when most of Edinburgh's inhabitants would still be in bed, presumably so as to limit the shame for John Livingston and his family.

At around 3am on Saturday 5 July, Jean was taken from her cell for execution at the Girth Cross of Holyrood in Canongate. The device to be used was the Maiden, a kind of gruesome guillotine which, while delivering a kinder death than being strangled and burnt, must have made a chilling sight, its blade glistening in the gloom as Jean stepped up to meet her fate. From the scaffold Jean delivered a repentant speech to the few who had managed to turn out to see the spectacle. She admitted 'the cruell murdering of mine own husband; which, although I did not with mine own hands, for I never laid mine hands upon him all the time that he was in murdering, yet I was the deviser of it and so the commiter!' Jean then lay her neck, 'sweetly and graciously in the place appointed, moving to and fro until she got a rest for her neck to lie in.' The executioner 'came behind her, and pulled out her feet, that her neck might be stretched out longer and so made more meet' for the stroke of the axe. At 4am her head was 'struck fra her bodie'. Meanwhile Janet Murdo who had, herself, confessed to her part in the murder, was burnt at the same time on the city's Castle Hill.

When news of the murder and arrests had first arrived in Edinburgh

Robert Weir had fled just as he had promised to do, though his plan to deflect guilt from Jean backfired. He managed to stay at large for four years before eventually being apprehended and brought to trial on 26 June 1604. Jean's testimony had presumably helped frame a case against him or at least helped elicit the confession on which his guilt was pronounced. Weir's crime was considered so grave that a rare punishment was called for. He would be 'broken on the wheel' (see page 22). Weir was lashed to a wooden wheel and then his arms and legs smashed with the coulter of a plough until he was dead. After this hideous punishment was carried out, Weir's body was left to hang on the wheel, which was placed between Warriston and the town of Leith, as a grim warning to others who might think of transgressing in a similar fashion.

A FAIR CRIMINAL BROKEN ON THE WHEEL.

Killer Robert Weir suffered a terrible form of punishment – being broken on the wheel. The practice is shown here from an illustration for the *Terrific Register, 1825*. (Copyright Look and Learn)

Chapter 30

Hacked to Pieces in a Muddy Lane
1602

At just after 8 o'clock in the morning on August 30, 1602, a maid's screams pierced the morning air in the sleepy little town of Market Rasen in Lincolnshire. She had been making her way to work down a muddy lane on the south side of the town when she was confronted by a horrifying sight in the track ahead of her. A wild looking man was desperately hacking at another with a sword. On hearing her cries, the culprit fled the scene, leaving his victim for dead.

The assault on the Reverend William Storre in the dying days of Elizabeth's reign was as vicious as any recorded in her forty-five year rule. It was the result of an argument which had broken out in the church where he was officiating. By all accounts Storre, in his early 40s, was a learned and respected man. He had attended Lincoln Grammar School before going up to Oxford University. After getting his MA he went on to become a fellow of Corpus Christi College. Here he spent twelve years in academia before deciding to take a position as curate in the Lincolnshire village of Boothby Graffoe. By 1597 he was vicar at Market Rasen.

During the year of 1602, tensions were running high in the community over the issue of enclosure, a process where wealthier landowners were fencing off common land for their own gain. The practice left many feeling their ancient rights were being trampled upon. Disputes over enclosure had been growing throughout England during the sixteenth century.

At Market Rasen, on one Sunday night in early August, things came to a head after evening prayers had been said in the church. A heated row broke out between several of the wealthier members of the town and some of the other inhabitants. Storre stepped in, suggesting that the church wasn't the place for such a debate. He recommended that the two sides should pick two or three men and adjourn to discuss the matter in a more civilised manner. However, some of those who had been arguing asked Storre which side he thought was in the right. The vicar was reluctant to be drawn, partly because he'd inevitably fall out with part of the community if he gave a view. But Storre was also worried because he'd previously had some problems with one of the men, Francis Cartwright, the 23-year-old son of a wealthy draper, Anthony Cartwright. A contemporaneous pamphlet published about the case reveals that 'no small unkindnesse had grown between them'. Francis, who was well known for his 'hotte stomacke' was on the side of the enclosing squire. However, repeatedly pressed to give his opinion, Storre eventually agreed. After hearing both the arguments he tended towards the side of the freeholders and against the 'Lords of the town'.

Storre's views, no doubt influential if not carrying any legal weight, left Francis Cartwright seething. He shouted out, 'The priest deserveth a good fee, he speaketh so like a lawyer.' and then continued to verbally abuse Storre. The next morning, Anthony Cartwright was discussing his son's behaviour with some neighbours when Francis interrupted them taking up where he left off in ranting abusively about Storre. The vicar, who, it seems, was among those in conversation, retorted to Francis that his derisive words would better describe himself. A furious Francis reached for his dagger and was narrowly restrained from stabbing Storre on the spot. Instead, he stormed into the nearby market place announcing to anyone who would listen that Storre was a 'scurvie, lowsie, paltrie Priest,' and that, 'whosoever said that hee was his friend, or spake in his cause, was a rogue and a rascall that he would … cut his throat, teare out his heart and hang his quarters on the may-pole.'

Storre was now so afraid of what Cartwright might do next that he went to see the local justice of the peace, asking for a 'recognizance', a Tudor version of an injuction or court order against Cartwright, which might make him keep his distance. Either reluctant to upset such a leading family, or feeling unable to make the order because Cartwright had not yet committed any actual crime, the JP in question vacillated, merely offering to bring Storre's complaints before the next quarter sessions in September.

In the meantime, Storre continued preaching sermons in his church while Cartwright sat in his family pew irritably writing down what was said. In the natural course of his sermons Storre delivered some 'sharpe and nipping reprehensions' to his flock. Cartwright was convinced that everything negative that Storre said was directed against him personally and his stomach 'filled with raw humours.'

A week later, Cartwright saw his chance for revenge after spotting Storre out and about on his own. He immediately went to a 'cutler's shop' where he picked up a short sword that he had taken to have sharpened. Rushing back to seek out Storre he caught up with the vicar. Storre turned around to see Cartwright approaching with his sword drawn and a crazed look on his face. Realising that there was no hope of escape, the terrified vicar decided to try and talk Cartwright out of attacking him, or as the pamphlet tells us to, 'assuage his passions.'

But Cartwright, 'being double armed, both with Force and Furie, would abide no parly.' Advancing on Storre he slashed at his target's left leg cutting deep into the flesh and almost completely severing the limb. As Cartwright delivered more frenzied blows with his weapon the unarmed Storre put up his arms in defence. This time the sword sliced off three of the vicar's fingers and 'gave him two grievous woundes on the outside of either arme between the elbow and the hand; the one in the middest of the arme' and the other cutting into the bone. Storre staggered backwards, falling into a puddle of water. He tried to get up, but as he did so the bones in his left leg snapped leaving his 'heele doubled backe to the calfe of his legge.' Even though his victim was no doubt writhing in agony Cartwright wasn't finished. He continued to hack away at Storre's body wounding him in the right thigh down to the bone and gashing his left knee.

It was at this point that the unwitting maid suddenly appeared, interupting the onslaught. Cartwright immediately halted his attack and ran off. Hearing the maid's cries of horror other townsfolk came running and were shocked to find their 'minister thus wallowed in the mire' with his blood 'extremely gushing out'. Some ran back to town crying 'murder'.

Despite suffering twenty-four separate wounds, Storre was still alive and his mangled body was carried to a nearby house where he was bandaged in an attempt to stop the bleeding. Several surgeons and 'bone-setters' were called to asses Storre's condition but they were in agreement that he was unlikely to survive his injuries, due to the extensive blood loss. Storre finally expired eight days later.

After the attack, Cartwright had run straight to his father's house, where a crowd assembled. Presumably, the maid had been able to identify Cartwright. In any case, the animosity he felt towards Storre was well known around the town and he was the obvious suspect. The elder Cartwright managed to keep the mob calm until the local constables arrived to arrest his only son. Cartwright was soon brought before a magistrate but, surprisingly, allowed to stay free on bail. He used this opportunity to flee to France before his case could come to trial.

This unsatisfactory state of affairs soon came to the attention of John Whitgift, the Archbishop of Canterbury, perhaps thanks to the efforts of Storre's widow (pregnant at the time of her husband's passing) who was determined to see justice done. The Privy Council got to hear of it too. The Lincolnshire JP and constable who had let Cartwright escape from their clutches were subsequently sacked.

Meanwhile, Cartwright turned up in the city of Rouen in Normandy, where he remained for six months, before signing up as a volunteer soldier serving under Sir Francis Vere in the Netherlands, the commander of English troops fighting against the Spanish. It may have been this 'service' that somehow enabled Cartwright's family and influential friends 'by corrupt dealing about His Majesty' to gain a pardon from the new monarch, James I, for the killing of Storre. Feeling that his life was no longer in peril, Cartwright was soon back in England.

What he and his allies hadn't taken into account was the steely character of Storre's widow. Her husband had been in debt at the time of his death and she and her five children had been forced to depend on the charity of the parish since his passing. She refused to accept the king's pardon as the final word in the case and travelled to London to 'sue for appeal'. In fact she spent the next five years trying to get the pardon overturned. A worried Cartwright tried to offer her money to drop the matter, but the widow Storre refused his offers.

The case had stirred up a good deal of feeling both locally and nationally and a whole host of local folk signed testimonies bemoaning Storre's murder at Cartwright's hands. Some of his former colleagues at Oxford University joined the clamour against what was perceived as a miscarriage of justice. Indeed, the whole pamphlet about the case that was printed on the anniversary of Storre's death may have been written at their instigation. Published in Oxford, its campaigning tone was a case for the prosecution including detailed evidence and witness statements.

Cartwright later recalled, 'Scarce was I entertained at home' but 'another affliction arose to endanger mee. The wife of the slaine sueth and appeale against me, notwithstanding my pardon.' For a time it looked like the widow Storre might be successful, the king himself indicating that if a legal problem was found with the granting of Cartwright's pardon, he should be hanged for the murder but the appeal was ultimately rejected on a point of law. Cartwright was bound over for five years and forced to make his peace with the Church by making an act of contrition. In effect, he became a free man, though one with a heavily tarnished reputation.

Cartwright returned to live in the village of Nettleton just a few miles from Market Rasen and began courting a gentlewoman. His father now dead, Cartwright found himself with fewer friends. At one point, unhappy at his choice of bride, four men attacked him with halberds, leaving him seriously injured. However, the marriage went ahead and Cartwright became a father to two children.

He seems to have been incapable of staying out of trouble for long. In 1611, he ended up in a confrontation with a Master Riggs at Grantham. According to his own account, Riggs attacked him with a sword and he was forced to kill his assailant in self-defence. This time Cartwright was convicted of manslaughter and imprisoned for a year, a relatively lenient sentence.

On gaining his freedom, Cartwright found himself in debt and left the country once more, this time volunteering to serve as a sailor on the *Vanguard* with Sir Richard Hawkins on a mission to Algiers to tackle pirates. Unfortunately for Cartwright, his reputation sailed with him and superstitious seafarers soon had him transferred to another ship which itself was then captured by the Algerians. Bad luck seemed to follow Cartwright everywhere and he was eventually forced to give up his life at sea and return to England.

By 1621 Cartwright had obviously achieved some kind of bizarre notoriety. The Storre case had also passed into legend and was still well known enough for Cartwright to decide it was time to make a kind of public confession. In effect *The Life, Confession and Heartie Repentance of Francis Cartwright, Gentleman: For his bloudie sinne in killing of one Master Storr* was not so much a mea cupla but a memoir. He could not quite bring himself to admit murder. While acknowledging that he had killed the vicar he says that he had only meant to give his adversary a 'slight wounding'. He goes on to excuse his actions by pleading that if

Storre had only moderated his language towards him the incident would not have happened.

Cartwright ends his account by revealing how, when he arrived back in England from his nautical adventures at the port of Deal in Kent, he nearly accidentally killed himself with his own sword while getting out of the coach on his way to Chatham. We do not know when or how Cartwright did finally die, but as he himself admitted that this would have been rather a fitting end to a very odd life.

Chapter 31

A Pair of Child Murderers
Caught at Last
1602

According to legend, Elizabeth I was sitting under an oak tree in the grounds of Hatfield Palace in Hertfordshire when she was told that she was to become queen. The princess had grown up at the palace and had returned to live there by November 1558 when the news came of the death of her half-sister Mary. In the penultimate year of Elizabeth's reign, nearly half a century after she was told she had ascended to the throne, grave news of death was once again doing the rounds in Hatfield. This time it involved the murder of a young child, a despicable crime where the suspects were identified almost immediately. Yet the perpetrators were not brought to justice until after the old queen was long dead and then, in the most sensational circumstances, by a girl who also happened to be called Elizabeth.

Court records show that on the 1st August 1606 a widow called Agnes Dell and her son George, a baker, were brought before the Hertford assizes accused of a bloody murder, one which had occurred four years earlier on 4 July, 1602. In the aftermath of what must have been a sensational case at the time, two popular pamphlets were speedily published revealing the details of how the Dells had come to be in the dock. One was called *The Horrible Murder of a Young Boy* while the other was entitled *The Most Cruell and Bloody Murther Committed by an Inkeepers Wife, called Annis Dell and her Sonne George Dell*. When it comes to details of the case the two accounts vary, but the essence of the story is the same. From the latter report we learn that at some time in early 1602, a rich yeoman called Anthony James and his wife Elizabeth, who lived in Essex, were targeted by a gang of thieves. All the household's servants were away, leaving only the couple and their two children – a boy and a girl – in the house. After breaking in, the robbers ransacked the place and then murdered the couple with their daggers, but could not bring themselves to do away with the youngsters too and carried them off instead. According to the former account the boy, a redhead, was aged three and the girl was four but the other report indicates that they are older.

Arriving in Hatfield, then called Bishops Hatfield, twenty miles north of London the criminals halted at an inn, run by Annis Dell (Annis being the Medieval form of the name Agnes). Once lodged at the inn the criminals offered Agnes a share of their booty if she would advise them on what to do with the children, who were also called Anthony and Elizabeth after their parents. It may be that Dell's establishment was already known to them as a safe place in which to hide or fence goods, roles often played by drinking establishments in Tudor England. Agnes Dell told the gang that the boy, Anthony, should be killed and that the girl, Elizabeth should have her tongue cut out. According to *The Horrible Murder* she swore three times to her villainous visitors never to tell anyone about the matter.

Over the next few hours, as the party got drunk, the children were seen by both a local labourer, Nicholas Deacon and a tailor called Henry Whilpley who took notice of the red-headed lad as he was particularly taken by the boy's expensively made green coat.

However, by the next day the children had disappeared. In *The Most Cruell and Bloody Murther* we learn that the children had been brought down during the night and that the girl had been left with Agnes and George, her son, while two robbers stuffed cow dung in Anthony's mouth then heartlessly slit his throat in the yard behind the inn. George then helped tie his body to a stake and led the thieves to a pond a mile out of the town. Agnes followed with Elizabeth in tow. The men threw Anthony's corpse in the pond. Then Agnes violently grabbed Elizabeth held open the girl's jaw and cut out her tongue with a knife. She even forced the poor child to throw the bloodied piece of flesh in the pond after her brother. According to *The Horrible Murder* Elizabeth was then abandoned in the hollow stump of a tree. In the official record it is George Dell, not the robbers, who was said to have been responsible for cutting Anthony's throat.

Three weeks later, some men were hunting wild fowl near the pond when their dogs picked up the scent of the dead body, which was soon dragged out. Presumably an inquest followed because we learn that both

Deacon and Whilpley recognised the boy's coat, which had been exhibited locally to see if anybody recognised it. They testified that they had seen him at the Dell's inn. Agnes Dell was sent for by the local justice, Sir Henry Butler, but denied knowledge of the children. Nevertheless the air of suspicion lingered over her and she was bound over to answer at the next assizes.

In fact, for the next four years, Dell and her son were brought before the assizes more than once but on each occasion no new evidence having come to light, it was found that there was no case against them to be heard. Meanwhile 'Mother Dell' who had been in debt, now seemed to have come into money and spent significant sums improving her property. As the Lent assizes of 1606 became due it appeared that the case would be dismissed once and for all.

In the hours after her ordeal, Elizabeth had been found by a pedlar and spent the next few years begging from place to place. Finally, however, she had found herself back in Hatfield and, suddenly recognising the Dell's inn, began shrieking. The 'extraordinarie noyse' she was making soon drew a crowd. The child's exhortations only got louder when Dell and her son appeared on the scene. Whilpley the tailor also came out to see what all the fuss was about and recognised the girl as having been with the missing boy at the Dell's place. Taken inside Dell's property Elizabeth also seemed to gesture that she knew the old layout of the house, before the Dells had improved it. Suspicions again being aroused about the Dells, the girl was brought before the local justices. When they discovered that she'd had her tongue cut out they questioned her as best they could with hand gestures. When Elizabeth was shown Anthony's coat, which had been kept, she was overcome with emotion and refused to be parted from it. Examined by the justices once more the Dells remained 'obstinate' and denied ever having seen the girl before.

The case was now the 'only table talk in the country' but since Elizabeth could not speak, no indictment could be drawn up against the Dells. Then, we are told, something strange occurred. Elizabeth, who had been taken into the care of the parish, was playing with another girl when a cock crowed. The other girl began crying 'cock-a-doodle-doo' and then, summoning her strength so did Elizabeth. Her friend ran home to spread the news saying: 'The dumb girl can speak'. The news spread like wildfire. Having regained the power of speech she was again brought before Sir Henry Butler, and was able to explain to him everything that had happened. He asked her who had cut out her tongue and she said, 'the olde woman and her sonne, that killed her brother and put her into the tree.' Then he asked her who had brought her to the old woman's house and she said, 'a man and a woman that had killed her father and her mother and taken a great bagge of money from them.' Elizabeth added that, 'the man and woman had given a great deale of that money to the olde woman and that the old woman did at that time did lift up her hands three times and did sweare three times that she would never tell anybody who they were.'

Stiffly examined by several other justices the authorities were now satisfied enough by her tale to bring the Dells to trial. The surviving court records reveal that they were both indicted for murder and that 'at Hatfield they assaulted Anthony James.' George Dell was alleged to have, 'cut his throat with a knife (worth 1d) and threw his body into a pond.'

Agnes and George Dell pleaded not guilty but, together with the testimony of Elizabeth as well as Whilpley, Deacon and others they were found guilty and sentenced to be hanged. The pair were put to death on 4 August 1606.

A tale of a girl who has had her tongue cut out, yet manages to speak may sound fantastical. It's certain that some elements of the story, as told in the pamphlets, has been embellished. In them, her seemingly miraculous ability to utter words is credited to divine intervention. Yet there are several sources for this story and it's not particularly unusual for a child who has witnessed something deeply traumatic to have lost the power of speech temporarily through the experience. Perhaps the injury to her tongue was not as extreme as the accounts would have us believe or was an exaggerated detail. Yet there is little doubt when comparing the pamphlets to the official legal records that the tracts were based on real and extraordinary, events.

Select Bibliography

ABBOTT, Geoffrey, *Execution: A Guide to the Ultimate Penalty*, (Summersdale, 2012)

ANDREWS, William, *Bygone Punishments*, (London, W Andrews and co, 1899)

AUBREY, John, *'Brief Lives,'* (Clarendon, 1898)

BAKER, Sir John, *The Oxford History of the Laws of England Volume VI: 1483-1558*, (OUP, 2003)

BELLAMY, John, *Strange, Inhuman Deaths: Murder in Tudor England*, (The History Press, 2005)

BELLAMY, John, *The Criminal Trial in Later Medieval England* (University of Toronto Press, 1998)

BERNARD, G., *The King's Reformation*, (Yale University Press, 2007)

BERNARD, G., *The Late Medieval English Church*, (Yale University Press, 2012)

BOTOLPH, Charles, *The History of the Noble House of Stourton in the County of Wilts* (1899)

BROADWAY, Jan, *Aberrant Accounts (Midland History, vol 33, 2008,)*

CALDERWOOD, David, *History of the Kirk of Scotland*, (Wodrow Society, 1842)

COCKBURN, J.S, *Calendar of Assize Records: Elizabeth I and James I: Introduction* (HMSO, 1985)

COCKBURN, J.S, *Calendar of Assize Records: Hertfordshire Indictments, Elizabeth I*, (PRO, 1975)

COCKBURN, J.S, *Calendar of Assize Records:Surrey Indictments, Elizabeth I* (PRO, 1980)

COCKBURN, J.S, *Calendar of Assize Records: Kent Indictments, Elizabeth I*, (PRO, 1979)

COCKBURN, J.S, *Calendar of Assize Records: Essex Indictments, Elizabeth I*, (PRO, 1978)

COCKBURN, J.S. (ed) *Crime in England, 1550-1800*, (Princeton University Press, 1977)

COCKBURN, J.S., *Patterns of Violence in English Society: Homicide in Kent 1560-1985* (Past and Present, vol 130, 1991)

COCKBURN, J.S., (ed) *Calendar of Assize Records: Sussex Indictments, Elizabeth I* (PRO, 1975)

COUZENS, Tim, *Hand of Fate*, (ELSP, 2001)

DORAN, Susan, *Elizabeth I and Her Circle* (OUP, 2015)

DOWLING, Maria, *Fisher of Men*, (Macmillan, 1999)

DUGDALE, Sir William, *Antiquities of Warwickshire*, (Thomas Warren, 1656)

FRASER, Antonia, *Mary Queen of Scots*, (Weidenfeld & Nicolson, 1969)

GASKILL, Malcolm, *Crime and Mentalities in Early Modern England*, (Cambridge University Press, 2000)

GUNN, S., and ROBINSON, W., *The Early Life of William Herbert, Earl of Pembroke*, (Welsh History Review, vol 18, 1997).

GURR, T., *Historical Trends in Violent Crime* (Crime and Justice, vol 3, 1981)

GUY, John, *My Heart is My Own: The Life of Mary Queen of Scots*, (Harper Perennial, 2004)

GRISTWOOD, Sarah *Elizabeth and Leicester* (Bantam, 2007)

GWYNN, Peter, *The King's Cardinal*, (Pimlico, 1992)

HALL, Edward, *Hall's Chronicle*, (J.Johnson, 1809)

HILTON, Lisa, *Elizabeth: Renaissance Prince* (Weidenfeld & Nicolson, 2015)

HOLDEN, Anthony, *William Shakespeare: The Man Behind the Genius* (Little, Brown, 2000)

HONAN, Park, *Christopher Marlowe: Poet and Spy* (OUP, 2007)

HUNNISETT, R., *Sussex Coroners' Inquests, 1485-1558,* (PRO, 1996)

HUNNISETT, R., *Sussex Coroner's Inquests 1558-1603*, (PRO, 1996)

HUTCHINSON, Robert, *The Last Days of Henry VIII*, (Weidenfeld & Nicolson, 2009)

HYDE, Patricia, *Thomas Arden in Faversham*, (Faversham Society, 1996)

JAMES, M.E., *The Murder at Cocklodge* (Durham University Journal, vol 57, 1965)

KESSELRING, K., *Mercy and Authority in the Tudor State*, (Cambridge University Press, 2008)

KURIYAMA, Constance Brown, *Christopher Marlowe: A Renaissance Life* (Cornell University Press, 2002)

LANGBEIN, John H., *Prosecuting Crime in the Renaissance*, (Harvard University Press, 1974)

LOVELL, Mary S., *Bess of Hardwick*, (Little, Brown, 2005)

MACHYN, Henry, *The Diary of Henry Machyn*, (Camden Society, 1848) MACMILLAN, Ken, *Stories of True Crime in Tudor and Stuart England* (Routledge, 2015)

MACNAMARA, F.N, *Memorials of the Danvers Family*, (Hardy & Co, 1985)

MALCOLM, Joyce Lee, *Guns and Violence*, (Harvard University Press, 2004)

MARSHBURN, Joseph H., *A Cruell Murder Donne in Kent*, (*Studies in Philology, vol 46, 1949*)

MARSHBURN, Joseph H., *Blood and Knavery*, (Fairleigh Dickinson University Press, 1975)

MAYHEW Graham, *Tudor Rye*, (University of Sussex, 1987)

MCKENZIE, Andrea, *This Death Some Strong and Stout Hearted Man Doth Choose*, (Law and History Review, vol 23, 2005,)

NEAVE, David, (ed) *Tudor Market Rasen*, (University of Hull, 1985)

NICHOLL, CHARLES. *The Reckoning: The Murder of Christopher Marlowe*, Vintage, 2002

NICHOLS, John Gough, *Chronicle of the Grey Friars of London*, (Camden Society, 1852)

PENNANT, Thomas, *Tour in Wales Volume 2,* (Cambridge University Press, 2014)

PITCAIRN, Robert, *Ancient Criminal Trials in Scotland*, (Bannatyne Club, 1833)

POGUE, Kate, *Shakespeare's Friends* (Praeger, 2006)

RANDALL, Martin, *Women, Murder, and Equity in Early Modern England*, (Routledge, 2007)

REID, Rachel Robertson, *The King's Council in the North* (Hardpress, 2012)

ROUGHEAD, William, *Twelve Scots Trials* (William Green & Sons, 1913)

ROWSE., A.L, *Shakespeare the Man,* (Harper, 1973)

RUFF, Julius R., *Violence in Early Modern Europe 1500-1800* (Cambridge University Press, 2001)

SAMAHA, Joel, *Hanging for a Felony* (The Historical Journal, vol 21, 1978)

SANDERSON, Margaret H.B., *Cardinal of Scotland*, (Donald, 2001)

SHARPE, James A., *Crime in Early Modern England 1550-1750*, (Longman, 1999)

SKELTON, Douglas, *Bloody Valentine: Scotland's Crimes of Passion*, (Black & White, 2004)

SKELTON, Douglas, *Deadlier Than the Male, (*Black & White, 2003)

SKIDMORE, Chris, *Death and the Virgin*, (Weidenfeld & Nicolson, 2011)

SPIERENBURG, Peter, *A History of Murder* (Polity Press, 2008)

STRYPE, John, *Ecclesiastical Memorials* (Clarendon Press, 1822)

SUGDEN, John, Sir Francis Drake (Pimlico, 2006)

TROW, M.J and TROW, Taliesin, *Who Killed Kit Marlowe?* (Sutton, 2001)

WEATHERFORD, John, *Crime and Punishment in the England of Shakespeare and Milton*, (McFarland & Co, 2001)

WEBB, Simon, *Execution*: *A History of Capital Punishment in Britain,* (The History Press, 2011)

WEIR, Alison, *Mary Queen of Scots and The Murder of Lord Darnley,* (Jonathan Cape, 2003)

WHITTINGTON-EGAN, Molly, *Classic Scottish Murder* (Neil Wilson, 2012)

WRIOTHESLEY, Charles, *A Chronicle of England During the Reigns of the Tudors*, (Camden Society, 1875)

Index

INDEX